FERGUSON
CAREER BIOGRAPHIES

DENZEL
WASHINGTON
Actor

James Robert Parish

Ferguson
An imprint of Facts On File

Denzel Washington: Actor

Ferguson
An imprint of Facts On File, Inc.
132 West 31st Street
New York NY 10001

Library of Congress Cataloging-in-Publication Data

Parish, James Robert.
   Denzel Washington, actor / James Robert Parish.
     p. cm.
   Includes bibliographical references and index.
   ISBN 0-8160-5829-6 (hc: alk. paper)
  1. Washington, Denzel, 1954– 2. Actors—United States—Biography. I. Title.
   PN2287.W452P37 2005
   791.4302'8'092—dc22
                                     2004012154

CONTENTS

1

A MAN WITH A PURPOSE

At the 74th Annual Academy Awards ceremony on March 24, 2002, veteran performer Sidney Poitier, the first African-American actor to win a Best Actor Oscar (for 1963's *Lilies of the Field*), received an honorary Oscar "for his extraordinary performances and unique presence on the screen" and for "representing the motion picture industry with dignity, style, and intelligence throughout the world." The award was presented by Denzel Washington. Later that evening, Halle Berry became the first African-American woman to win a Best Actress Oscar (for her performance in *Monster's Ball*). That same night, Denzel Washington strode to the podium to receive a Best Actor Oscar for his role as a rogue cop in the thriller *Training Day*.

Washington was the first African American to win the Academy Award for Best Actor since Poitier's Oscar victory in 1963. Acknowledging this very important accomplishment, Washington good-naturedly told the audience, "Forty years I've been chasing Sidney, and what do they do? They give him one on the same night. But there's nothing I'd rather do, sir."

An Actor's Actor

Denzel Washington does not want to be known as a black actor. Although he is extremely proud of his black heritage and appreciative of the growing opportunities for racial minorities in post-1960s Hollywood, he would rather be known as an actor. As he once explained to the *Los Angeles Times*, "Black is not all I am. That's my cultural historical background, my genetic makeup, but it's not all of who I am, nor is it the basis from which I answer every question."

In shaping his screen career, Denzel has frequently rejected lucrative parts that may have pigeonholed him in stereotypical ethnic roles (e.g., pimps, drug addicts, gangsters). Instead, Denzel has sought out acting parts that are *not* color specific, such as the investigative reporter in *The Pelican Brief* (1993) or the quadriplegic homicide detective in *The Bone Collector* (1999). This ambitious actor has been determined to utilize his acting talents and good looks to become a versatile leading man. He has become known in the filmmaking industry and to the filmgoing public as a fine performer, and not one qualified by the color of his skin.

However, in his more than 20 years of filmmaking, Denzel has not shied away from playing roles written specifically for African-American characters. He has taken several of these roles because of the creative challenges that they presented. He has played a South African martyr in *Cry Freedom* (1987); an ex-slave who joins the Union Army in the Civil War story *Glory* (1989), a part for which he won a Best Supporting Actor Oscar; an ill-fated championship boxer in *The Hurricane* (1999); and an African-American high-school football coach fighting for the integration of his squad in *Remember the Titans* (2000).

Over the years Washington has also often teamed with distinguished black filmmaker Spike Lee for African American–themed film projects: *Mo' Better Blues* (1990), *Malcolm X* (1992), and *He Got Game* (1998). Then in the feature film *Antwone Fisher* (2002), the first film that Denzel directed, he chose to tell the true-life story of a young black sailor whose emotional problems were the by-products of a troubled childhood. Denzel also produced and co-starred in the film.

Denzel is a dedicated craftsman who believes "I'm not a movie star in my own perception, I'm an actor. *Movie star* belongs to the people, not to me." Washington is a very private man who shies away from media attention.

Nevertheless, he insists, "I think I'm a lot more open about my private life than some people in this business. I may not be an open book, but I think people know as much about me as they need to know."

Although named by *People* magazine as one of Hollywood's "Most Beautiful People" and the "Sexiest Man Alive," 6-foot, 185-pound Denzel is cautious about what his characters will do on screen. He has always been awkward about movie love scenes and has refused to do any on-camera disrobing. He explains, "I am a little old-fashioned . . . I believe less is more." The modest man also reasons, "Do I think people want to hear me say I'm sexy? Why do you want me to say it myself? It's *embarrassing.*"

Publicity-shy Washington is also levelheaded about his high standing in the film industry. He acknowledges, "It's always been a nice, steady climb for me, and I feel pretty lucky about that." Yet he candidly says of his professional training and his shrewd role-picking, "Luck is where opportunity meets preparation."

Part of Denzel's success as a screen star is due his reputation as an actor's actor. Martin Stellman, who guided Denzel through the British-made *For Queen and Country* (1988), observed, "He's almost minimalist in his expressions and gestures and movement, yet he still manages to be powerful and charismatic on the screen." Another film-maker, Edward Zwick—who directed Washington in such features as 1989's *Glory* and 1996's *Courage under Fire* and —has said, "Working with an actor like Denzel is like steering a Maserati compared to steering a Dodge. You don't have to crank the wheel—you make an adjustment of two degrees, and he takes off like a shot, coming up with something original and fresh."

Distinguished actor Morgan Freeman, who co-starred with Denzel in *Glory*, has remarked that Washington does incredible amounts of research to burrow into a screen characterization. "He's intimidating that way," Freeman details. "When Denzel gets there he's there, but he arrives there by a lot of effort."

A Religious Family Man

While Washington is highly career-oriented—often to the point of being a workaholic—he has not allowed his superstar status to overwhelm his perspective on life. His two biggest grounding forces are his family (his long-time wife Pauletta and their four children) and his religion. As the son of a Pentecostal minister, Denzel has strong religious beliefs and practices, which include reading the *Daily Word* (a monthly publication offering daily spiritual inspiration and practical help through inspirational

Denzel holds the Academy Award for Best Actor, which he received for his role in Training Day. (Associated Press)

stories and prayer) and weekly churchgoing. He has said, "God is my hero."

Wanting to share his financial good fortune, Washington—who commands $20 million per film—devotes a good deal of time and money to worthy charities, especially those that support the black community. His causes of choice have included the Boys and Girls Clubs of America, Nelson Mandela's Children's Fund, and a $2.5 million gift to rebuild the West Angeles Church of God in Christ (which the Washingtons attend).

2

BEGINNINGS

Denzel Washington Jr. was born on December 28, 1954, in Mount Vernon, New York, a middle-class community just north of Manhattan. Denzel (pronounced Den-ZELL) was the second of three children (he has an older sister, Lorice, and, a younger brother, David) of Reverend Denzel Washington and his wife, Lennis.

Denzel's father, a Pentecostal minister from Virginia, worked two jobs to help support his family. He was employed at the local water utility company and at S. Klein, a department store. On Sundays, he preached to his congregation, which often consisted only of family members and one or two other parishioners. Denzel's mother, originally from Georgia, was a former gospel singer who operated a beauty parlor that eventually grew into a chain of shops.

In the still racially segregated United States of the mid-1950s, Mount Vernon was an unusual town, where a racially mixed population of locals lived in relative harmony. When

Denzel later recalled growing up in Mount Vernon, he described: "My friends were West Indians, blacks, Irish, Italians, so I learned a lot of different cultures." Said the actor, "It was a good background for someone in my business." He has termed his hometown "the safest and best community on the planet."

Guiding Influences

The Washingtons led a financially stable existence, thanks to the parents' strong work ethic, which they instilled in their children as well. Because of the Reverend's two jobs, he left home early in the morning and didn't return until late at night. As a result, Denzel and his siblings saw little of their father during the week and never really got to know him as a person. However, on Sundays, at the Reverend's church, the children experienced their father's passionate sermonizing, which created a strong religious base in their lives.

As a clergyman, Denzel Sr. had a strong sense of morality. He kept tight control over outside influences that might affect his children. In the Washington household, swearing, drinking, and smoking were strictly forbidden. Denzel Sr. also believed that many Hollywood movies displayed loose morals, and he decided what films his children could watch. As a result, except for the few occasions when they sneaked off to see an action picture at a local cinema, the Washington children were limited to viewing religious epics such as *King of Kings* (1961) or Disney animated features.

The equally hard-working Mrs. Washington provided the children with daily guidance. Denzel later admitted that she was an effective authority figure who, like her exacting husband, believed in strict discipline. Whenever Denzel was tempted to do anything wrong, he knew that if he took such a misstep "my mother would kill me!" That deterrent helped to keep Denzel and his siblings out of major scrapes.

One of Denzel's favorite childhood haunts was the Boys Club in Mount Vernon, which he began attending when he was just six years old. There he could safely hang out and talk with friends, play basketball and football, plan camping trips, and so forth. Denzel's mentor at the Boys Club was the Club's director, Billy Thomas. Washington—now a national spokesperson for the Boys and Girls Clubs—says it was Thomas "who taught by example and challenged me to achieve my potential in life." Denzel adds, "I know that without his guidance and direction I would not be where I am today."

Washington also acknowledges the role of one of the Club's counselors, Charles White. Denzel explains, "To do anything, you have to believe in yourself. Somebody has to give you that encouragement. Charles White was always telling us, 'You can do anything you want!' That stuck." (As Denzel grew into a teenager, he would become a counselor's aide at the Club's summer camp.)

By the time Denzel was 10 years old, he was part of a new busing program to promote racial integration. He and his siblings now attended classes at a school on the other side of town. Although their new school was largely white, Denzel never felt out of place because his parents had taught him and his siblings to always be proud.

When Denzel was 12, his daily routine also included working part time at a local barbershop that his mother co-owned. There he would help clean up, use the whisk broom on customers after a haircut, or run errands, such as taking patrons' clothes to a nearby cleaner. Washington grew to love the tips he received for his efforts, leading him to say, "Everybody looked like a dollar bill to me." This work experience, which allowed him to earn his own spending money, gave him a sense of independence. The job also taught him the value and power of money, lessons that have remained with him throughout life.

Already good-looking, the fast-growing Denzel was a good athlete and was becoming the object of girls' attention. However, he was extremely shy (and especially self-conscious about the gap between his two front teeth), so he was generally unaware of his appeal to the opposite sex.

A Family Calamity

When Denzel was 14, his relatively serene world col-lapsed. His parents split and soon divorced, with his father returning to Virginia. The trauma of the divorce shook Denzel to the core. In reaction, he said later, "I rejected everything," including religion. The once well-mannered youth became unmanageable. He began asso-ciating with disreputable characters and was full of such rage that, as he has recalled, he began "beating people up in school."

While Denzel was definitely out of control, his upbring-ing—especially his mother's influence—and good luck prevented him from getting into confrontations with the police or into other major trouble that could have handi-capped him. "My mother stuck by me so much. She would come out in the street and embarrass me. We'd be out there arguing in the street and she would come and get me."

As Washington further described, "When it came down to the moment of should I go this way or do that, I'd think about her and say, 'Nah, let me get myself outta here before I get into trouble.' I think I was more of an actor even back then." Washington admits, "I was in situations as a teenager where I could have easily ended up doing a lot of time. That wasn't my fate. God had another plan for me, so I'm thankful."

In retrospect, Washington also acknowledges that his mom "saw to it I was exposed to a lot of [positive, cultural] things. She couldn't afford it, but she was very intelligent. She is basically responsible for my success."

A Timely Intervention

Desperate to remedy the problems in her single-family household, Mrs. Washington scraped together enough funds—bolstered by financial scholarships—to enroll her two older children in boarding schools. Denzel was sent to Oakland Academy, a prep school in upstate New York. In this largely white school, the 100 students were required to wear jackets and neckties to classes.

Still confused by the breakup of his parents' marriage and ill at ease in his new environment, Denzel put little effort into his class work, and didn't mind that he was an academic underachiever. He channeled his energies into playing sports: basketball, baseball, football, and track, as well as participating in a local band for which he played piano. (Washington's biggest thrill in his Oakland Academy years was when his long-absent father attended the big football game in Denzel's senior year.) For a while, Denzel envisioned himself one day becoming a professional athlete.

By the time Washington graduated from Oakland Academy in 1972, he was still unsure what he wanted to do with his life. On the other hand, he knew he needed a college education to properly prepare himself for the future. Of the colleges he applied to, Yale University turned him down, and Boston University accepted him, but his grades were insufficient for a much-needed financial scholarship. As a result, Denzel enrolled at Fordham University, whose Bronx campus was not far away from his mother's home. He paid for his tuition through scholarships and such after-school jobs as operating a babysitting service at a Greek Orthodox church in Manhattan.

Washington began his studies at Fordham in the fall of 1972 as a pre-med major, a choice made to please his mother. He also played on the football team but soon became discouraged when a new gridiron coach demoted him from playing defensive back to second string and benchwarmer. As the school year progressed, Denzel realized he did not have the aptitude or drive for the demanding career of medicine. This realization led him to switch to journalism. However, even with a new major and the diversion of playing on the basketball team, Denzel remained listless about his course work and frequently skipped classes. His grade point average badly suffered. When he was about to flunk out of school at the end of his first semester of his sophomore year, Mrs. Washington convinced campus authorities to let her son take time off, to hopefully regain his perspective on life and the value of education.

A Needy Reevaluation

Cast adrift from his academic routine, Denzel found work where he could. For a while, he was employed in the municipal sanitation department as a garbage collector, then at a post office. Finding these jobs unfulfilling, he considered joining the Army but never went through with it. Eventually, Washington opted to reenroll at Fordham.

In the summer before returning to the university, he accepted a job at a YMCA camp in Lakeville, Connecticut. He was hired to supervise the camp's sports program and to help organize talent shows. For one such evening's entertainment, Denzel and the other counselors put together a program for the campers. Doing his bit in the proceedings, Washington found that not only did the audience respond to his performance (a recitation), which showed a great deal of natural presence, but he also felt very much at ease on the stage. It led him to a sudden realization that acting was what he wanted to do with his life.

Once back at Fordham, Washington spent most of his succeeding semesters at the university's Manhattan campus pursuing both his journalism studies (as a job option to fall back on in future times of need), writing poetry, and taking drama courses. Among his classes was a theater workshop taught by Robinson Stone, an English/dramatic literature professor whose professional acting had included working on stage in a production of *Othello* with the legendary actor Paul Robeson and having a role in the World War II prisoner-of-war movie *Stalag 17* (1953). At one of the first sessions of Stone's workshop, the instructor asked his students what their professional goals were. Denzel blurted out that he wanted to be "the greatest actor in the world."

Before long, Stone realized that Washington's boast was not out of the realm of possibility, as the young man showed a natural bent for performing. As Denzel learned basic acting techniques, his verve for life and his craft grew, and he took more interest in his academics. Washington remembers, "At last something was exciting to me. It was like I had found my niche. Suddenly, college took on a new meaning."

Mentoring this newcomer actor, the teacher cast Denzel in the title role of a campus production of Eugene O'Neill's *The Emperor Jones*. Denzel did so well in this demanding project that, in his senior year, Stone gave him the lead role in Shakespeare's *Othello*. Fired up with enthusiasm and passion for acting, Denzel said, "I enjoyed being out in front of people. I enjoyed the way they responded to me."

Stone was so pleased with his protégé's creative interpretation of *Othello* that he encouraged fellow actor/movie star José Ferrer to attend a performance. Stone recalled that he and Ferrer "agreed that Denzel had a brilliant career ahead of him." Acclaimed for his acting achievements on campus, it was not long before someone said to Denzel, "You can do this for a living." The professor agreed and soon arranged for TV and movie casting agents to come see Washington perform. It led to Washington signing with a talent agency.

Making His TV Debut

Shortly after his latest successful appearance on the Fordham University stage, the handsome young actor tested for a role in the television film *Wilma* (1977). The NBC-TV production dealt with African-American track sprinter Wilma Rudolph (played by Shirley Jo Finney) who overcame physical and personal handicaps to win a trio of gold medals at the 1960 Olympics. Denzel auditioned for the role of Wilma's boyfriend. Because he had no professional experience, he took the risky step of presenting the film's casting director with an exaggerated acting résumé. Years later, Washington laughingly recalled, "Maybe they cast me because I cared enough about it to lie to get it."

Soon after graduating from Fordham with a degree in journalism and drama, Denzel was in front of the cameras "and all I remember feeling was fear." In fact, the fledgling actor was so preoccupied with his new acting job (which required him to adjust from stage work to performing in front of a camera) that he took only momentary notice of another performer in the cast. She was North Carolina–born Pauletta Pearson, a young actress and musician, who had the role of runner Mae Faggs. Because Pauletta was just finishing her part in *Wilma* as Denzel was starting his, the two had little opportunity for any exchange beyond a quick hello. Caught up in his work, Denzel quickly forgot about her. However, the more professionally seasoned Pearson took full notice of attractive Denzel.

Wilma debuted on December 19, 1977. Despite high hopes for his career debut, the TV production came and went without too much notice. Denzel was disappointed by the tepid reaction to *Wilma*, but, by then, he was already enrolled in the American Conservatory Theatre (ACT) in San Francisco. Having seen an impressive ACT production of *The Taming of the Shrew* on PBS-TV, Washington was determined to go to the American Conservatory. One of thousands to audition for the prestigious school's three-year program, he was among the 45 selected for the difficult curriculum. However, as before, Washington showed little enthusiasm for classroom theory, only coming alive when he was performing in workshop productions like *Moonchildren* and *Man and Superman*. Soon believing that he had absorbed enough from acting technique lessons, he increasingly began to cut classes. He spent more of his time at his part-time waiter's job and hanging out in the Golden Gate city. Nevertheless, the twentysomething Washington, who now sported an Afro hairstyle and a goatee, was among the 20 ACT students who survived the academic cuts and was accepted into the second-year class.

Restless with the ACT regimen, Denzel chose to leave San Francisco. Since he was already on the West Coast, he went to Los Angeles, where he stayed with a cousin. He hoped he could break into the Hollywood film and television industry. However, the novice quickly discovered that in sprawling L.A. "not only do you need a car, you need a job."

Washington soon realized how fiercely competitive it was for a struggling newcomer in the late 1970s to gain a foothold in show business—especially for a black man. Disappointed and frustrated, Washington returned to New York and the safety net of his mother's apartment in Mount Vernon. His immediate plan was to find his professional niche in the theater world.

3

PAYING HIS DUES

For a young African-American actor such as Denzel, returning to New York in the late 1970s was fortuitous. For one thing, the United States was slowly becoming more racially integrated. This was especially true in the New York theater world. Finally, African Americans were being given more meaningful opportunities to participate in productions. No longer was black talent restricted to the few available racially stereotyped parts. Gradually, significant roles in integrated theater productions were becoming available to black actors. Meanwhile, several black acting troupes such as the Negro Ensemble Company continued to provide opportunities for African Americans to practice their craft in front of audiences.

In this period of growing civil rights for blacks, Denzel auditioned for and found roles in such off-Broadway projects as *The Mighty Gents, Spell #7,* A *Gee-chee Quick Magic*

Trance Manual, and Lonnie Elder III's *Ceremonies in Dark Old Men.* For a 1979 Shakespeare in the Park production of *Coriolanus*—staged by the Black and Hispanic Acting Ensemble—Washington played Aediles. While many of these modest presentations were short-lived, they provided Washington with needed theater experience. (To further hone his skills, he took acting classes with Wyn Handman, one of the pioneers of the off-Broadway theater movement.) However, there were frequent periods when Denzel had no acting assignments and he was forced to go on unemployment.

When Denzel was cast in the four-hour TV movie *Flesh and Blood,* he thought now he would make his professional mark on nationwide television. Washington played Kirk, who was involved in a young street tough's rise to the top of the boxing world. However, the CBS-TV network production, which aired in October 1979, did little for Denzel's career.

Meeting Ms. Right . . . Again

While Denzel was struggling through his acting apprenticeship in New York, he became reacquainted with Pauletta Pearson, whom he'd first met on the set of *Wilma* in 1977. Fate threw the two together (first at a mutual friend's party, then at a theater showcase performance), and they quickly began dating. Within a year, the couple was living together, sharing Denzel's room at his mother's apartment in Mount Vernon so that they could stretch their meager budget as far as possible.

During this trying professional period, it was Pauletta and his mother who gave Washington daily encouragement to continue in his chosen craft. Their support helped him to overcome the disappointments of unsuccessful auditions or short-lived productions. He was aware that, although things were improving for African Americans in the entertainment field, it was still difficult for a black performer to find steady, meaningful work in show business. At times, his ongoing career struggle made him bitter and angry.

In 1980 Denzel was cast in Sharon Pollock's *One Tiger to a Hill* performed at the Manhattan Theatre Club. Thereafter, no roles came along. A deeply disheartened Washington was ready to admit professional defeat and accept any type of work in order to support Pauletta and himself. He took a position with the county department of recreation. However, even at this point, Pauletta refused to become discouraged. She kept urging Denzel to "keep trying" to make a go of his acting career and he continued to audition. One week before he was to start his new job in the county department, he was cast in a key assignment in Laurence Holder's *When the Chickens Come Home to Roost*.

Denzel was to play Malcolm X in this fictional drama about a meeting between the black political activist and Elijah Muhammad, the head of the Nation of Islam. Washington had a difficult task ahead to learn all about his stage character since, as a child in his father's household, he had heard little or nothing about this assassinated champion for black rights. Burrowing into his role, he studied audio tapes and film footage of Malcolm X to better prepare for the upcoming production. He even dyed his hair red to look more like his stage alter ego.

When the Chickens Come Home to Roost opened off-Broadway at the New Federal Theatre on June 18, 1981. Although the show only lasted for 12 performances, it was long enough for Denzel to receive sterling reviews for his riveting interpretation of Malcolm X. The *New York Times'* Frank Rich praised Washington for being "honorable and altruistic without ever becoming a plaster saint." Later, the Audience Development Committee awarded Denzel the annual Audelco Award for his impressive acting.

Thrilled and uplifted by this artistic experience and his new knowledge of the slain black leader, Denzel had a premonition: "I know I'm going to do this movie [about Malcolm X] one day. I *know* it." He promised himself he "wasn't going to do anything even dealing with Malcolm X until I did the film about his life."

Breaking into the Movies

During this up-and-down period in Denzel's stage career, his talent agent arranged for Denzel to audition for an upcoming Hollywood film. The agent reasoned that it would be an opportunity for Denzel to earn a healthy paycheck, and the experience might open doors for the young actor within the film industry. The film in question was *Carbon Copy* (1981), which co-starred George Segal as a successful California executive who suddenly discovers he has a 17-year-old black son, the product of a long-forgotten relationship. Washington was hired for the movie, which ultimately failed to make much of an impact with filmgoers.

By the time of this latest professional setback, Denzel was emotionally better equipped to deal with failure and he needed little encouragement to pursue his true love—the theater. It also helped that, by then, he was already cast in Charles Fuller's *A Soldier's Play*, which focused on a World War II training-camp murder. Presented by the Negro Ensemble Company, the drama featured Washington (as Private 1st Class Melvin Peterson), Adolph Caesar, and Samuel L. Jackson. The show bowed at Manhattan's Theatre Four in November 1981 to great acclaim. The *New York Times* pointed out that Washington "who recently scored as Malcolm X in *When the Chickens Come Home to Roost*, is equally effective here as another, cooler kind of

Critics were impressed with Denzel's (fourth from left) performance in the off-Broadway production A Soldier's Play. *The play also featured the then-unknown actor Samuel L. Jackson (fifth from left).* (Photofest)

young renegade." The Hollywood trade paper *Variety* cited Denzel for being "particularly impressive."

A Soldier's Play won several awards, including the Pulitzer Prize. Denzel earned off-Broadway's Obie Award for his performance.

St. Elsewhere to the Rescue

While the screen comedy *Carbon Copy* had come and gone, one individual who saw the heavy-handed feature film was TV producer Bruce Paltrow (father of Oscar-winning actress Gwyneth Paltrow). He was assembling a large cast of regulars for *St. Elsewhere*, a new hour-long medical drama to debut on the NBC network in the fall of 1982. Despite the lure of a steady and healthy salary, Washington was quite concerned about committing himself to a full-time stint as a regular on a TV series. He feared being typecast (seen as able to play only one type of character) by appearing on a weekly series; he also felt it might hurt his future opportunities for stage and film assignments. Eventually, thanks to Paltrow's persistence, Denzel and his agent negotiated a deal that would allow Denzel time off to pursue other artistic options. Besides, Washington told himself, this series seemed an unlikely candidate for success and would probably only last for its initial 13-week network commitment.

On *St. Elsewhere*, Denzel was cast as Dr. Phillip Chandler, a member of the medical team at Boston's run-down St. Eligius Hospital. *St. Elsewhere* debuted on October 26, 1982, to strong critical praise for tackling difficult topics and for the cast's solid acting. While this medical drama never earned high home-audience ratings, it was a critical favorite, winning a dozen Emmys in its six years on the air.

When *St. Elsewhere* proved to be an ongoing TV project season after season, Paltrow and the production team kept their word that Denzel's Dr. Chandler would remain a secondary character in the series. As such, this handsome, well-mannered physician often disappeared for a few episodes here and there, and then quietly returned to the story line. Later, Washington candidly admitted, "I didn't

From 1982 to 1988, Denzel was part of the ensemble cast of St. Elsewhere, a television drama. (Photofest)

give a lot of input into my character, because I didn't want it to expand too much. I wanted to remain in the background so I could do movies." By the time the acclaimed television series ended its run in spring 1988, Denzel was earning $30,000 per episode.

A Soldier's Story

During Denzel's long tenure on *St. Elsewhere,* he stretched his talents in several directions. He wrote a few screenplays (about which he acknowledged "They're just not too good . . . other people told me they stunk, too."). He took time out from his TV series work to film the movie adaptation of *A Soldier's Play,* retitled *A Solder's Story* (1984), directed by Norman Jewison. Denzel recreated his role of Peterson, one of the men who had clashed with the homicide victim in the film. While *Newsweek* thought the film adaptation suffered from "its complexity [being] thinned out," *Variety* rated the entry "a taut, gripping film." The trade publication cited Washington as being "totally convincing" and Pauline Kael (*The New Yorker*) judged Denzel as "the standout" in the superior cast.

Meanwhile, Denzel made other forays into TV work. He was in the 1984 CBS network feature *License to Kill.* Cast as an assistant district attorney, he supported the lead characters in an account of a young woman killed by a drunk driver. Also for CBS, Washington starred in *The*

George McKenna Story (1986), a TV movie based on the true-life story of the crusading principal in a drug-infested South Los Angeles high school. Denzel's character inspires his students to care about their education. The film's director was a _St. Elsewhere_ co-star, Eric Laneuville. Denzel received far better reviews than the film did as a whole.

In the midst of his upward spiraling career, he and Pauletta married in June 1983 in her hometown of Newton, North Carolina. The following year, she gave birth to their first child, John David. (The Washingtons would later become parents of Katia in 1988 and of twins, Malcolm and Olivia, in 1991.) Becoming a parent gave work-obsessed Denzel a new slant on life. As he later analyzed it, the arrival of his first offspring made him start to realize "the difference between life and making a living. I used to think what I did for a living was my life. Acting [was] my life. When we had that first child, acting became making a living. The child was life. It's a miracle, an absolute miracle what happens." Meanwhile, to be a homemaker and mother, Pauletta had put her career in the arts on hold.

Building His Resume

In 1986, Denzel accepted a supporting role in the film _Power_. This assignment gave him the opportunity to work with veteran director Sidney Lumet and to interact with a distinguished cast that included Richard Gere, Julie Christie, and Gene Hackman. What especially appealed to Washington about the project was that his role—a slick lobbyist for rich Arab oil interests—had originally been written for a middle-aged white actor. Despite the high-caliber talent in this film, critics scorned it, saying the plot lacked a proper finale and that the script was often simplistic. But Denzel emerged from the film without receiving much criticism for his performance.

Usually Denzel waited to be approached for an acting assignment, but he was so intrigued by Oliver Stone's then-upcoming picture, *Platoon* (1986), that he campaigned hard to win the role of Sergeant Elias, a Native American member of the American forces fighting in Vietnam. Stone rejected Denzel for the pivotal role, even when Denzel pointed out that his background was part–Native American. Instead, Stone offered him another assignment in the combat picture, which Denzel turned down because he felt the role reflected poorly on the black soldiers who had served in Vietnam.

In contrast, Washington pondered for awhile before accepting his next screen assignment, *Cry Freedom* (1987). For this picture, British filmmaker Richard Attenborough was looking for "a man of charm, of erudition, of intellect, of perception, who was humorous, relaxed yet confident" to play the key screen role of Steve Biko. Biko was a real-life South African radical leader; he fought against apartheid, the South African government's rigid policy of racial segregation in all walks of life. After Biko had been banned from political activity in 1973 by the white South African government, he died mysteriously while in police custody. Attenborough was shown a tape of the movie *A Soldier's Story* and thought that Denzel fit the bill for the upcoming movie.

Washington was leery about taking on the job offer for several reasons. It meant he would have to commute between Zimbabwe (which is located northeast of South Africa) and the United States to fulfill his other professional obligations. He hated the notion of being separated from his wife and child. Also, Denzel was concerned about the film's point of view. To give the picture a wider audience, *Cry Freedom* focused on a white South African reporter who first opposes, then befriends, and later champions the memory of Biko. After much indecision, Denzel finally chose to make the film, reasoning, "The important thing to me was to give people a chance to find out who [Steve Biko] is. . . ."

With only several weeks to prepare for the part, Denzel began to extensively research the real-life character he was to portray on screen, studying photographs, audio tapes, and film footage of the late activist. To enhance his likeness to Biko, Washington embarked on a special diet to add 30 pounds to his frame, grew a straggly goatee, and worked with an instructor to develop an appropriate South African accent. To further augment his look as Biko, Washington had the caps over his front teeth temporarily removed, which revealed a wide gap.

When *Cry Freedom* was released in November 1987, critics complained that the film's white point of view was its downfall. Roger Ebert (*Chicago Sun-Times*) pointed out, "This movie promises to be an honest account of the turmoil in South Africa but turns into a routine cliff-hanger about the editor's flight across the border." Rita Kempley (*Washington Post*), while disturbed that the black characters had been submerged in the film, nevertheless found that Denzel gave "a zealous, Oscar-caliber performance."

Despite Washington's disappointment over the artistic outcome of this screen project, he did receive acclaim from his peers. He was nominated for (but did not win) both a Golden Globe Award and an Oscar for his performance. The film had also allowed Denzel to visit Africa for the first time. For the rising actor it felt, "like a homecoming" to be in the land of his ancestors and to learn more about his cultural roots. He added, "I'll never forget Africa. . . . I felt very comfortable there."

In 1988, Denzel made another a British-produced feature film, *For Queen and Country*. Having a lull in his workload and being fearful of unemployment, he had gotten hold of the film script and strongly pursued the director, Martin Stellman, for the central role; the filmmaker had initially been seeking a British black performer to take the part, but he ended up hiring Denzel. This time Washington worked with a speech coach and lived for a time in South London to help with the English accent needed for the part. In *For Queen and Country*, he was seen as an Afro-Caribbean man back home in London from fighting in the Falklands, where the British had defeated Argentina in the early 1980s. Released from military duty, the former paratrooper questions all his life values as he confronts racism, poverty, and corruption. The bleak tale was not released in the United States until 1989, and even then on just a few screens. Thus, relatively few moviegoers got to see Washington's seasoned performance in this picture.

Having been away from home and family too long, Denzel was happy to next accept a stage assignment—this time on Broadway.

4

A MARCH
TO GLORY

The production that finally brought Denzel Washington to Broadway was *Checkmates* by Ron Miller. The drama presented Denzel as a slick Detroit liquor distributor who lives with his wife in a two-story home shared with another couple. To research his role as a *buppie* (slang for black urban professional), Denzel worked with a real-life counterpart of his character so he could better understand his role—that of a seemingly charming man who is actually an abusive bigot.

The play opened in August 1988 and lasted for 177 performances. Critics and theatergoers alike were not especially impressed with the play. Nevertheless, in a cast of seasoned talent, Denzel received positive notice from reviewers.

If *Checkmates* had not been the artistic and commercial hit that Washington had hoped for, it did help him achieve a goal of every American stage actor—to perform on the Broadway stage.

Earning His First Oscar

Now that Denzel's lucrative six-year tenure on TV's _St. Elsewhere_ had come to an end, he was anxious to propel his screen career forward. His next film was MGM's _The Mighty Quinn_ (1989). In this whodunit he was cast in the lead role of Xavier Quinn, the black head of police on a picturesque Caribbean island. While investigating the murder of a white resort owner who had been killed because of a large sum of money, he becomes convinced that the chief suspect—his childhood friend (played by Robert Townsend, one of Denzel's coplayers in _A Soldier's Story_)—is innocent.

This comedic mystery allowed Denzel a well-rounded role. Not only did his on-screen alter ego actually have a love life (an aspect sadly missing from most movies of that time that dealt with black characters), but in one of the picture's lighter moments, he performs an impromptu reggae number. One sequence that did not make it into the film's release print was a kissing/seduction scene between Washington and the flirty white wife of the resort's manager. MGM felt that many filmgoers were not ready for interracial love scenes.

While _The Mighty Quinn_ did not make much money, Denzel received sizeable critical attention for his per-

formance. *People* maga-
zine enthused, "He gives a
small-time film some big-
time appeal." Roger Ebert
(*Chicago Sun-Times*) said,
"Washington is at the
heart of the movie, and
what he accomplishes is a
lesson in movie acting."
New York magazine's
David Denby said that
Washington "has a quick,
fluid intelligence, fierce
concentration, a beautiful
voice, and a graceful way
of taking the obvious
macho emphasis out of an

In the film Glory, *Denzel portrayed a soldier in the first all-black Civil War regiment.* (Photofest)

action role." Denby predicted, "Sooner or later Denzel
Washington will become a great movie star."

From the comedic *The Mighty Quinn* Washington moved
on to *Glory* (1989), the first of several movies he would
make with director Edward Zwick. *Glory* unfolded the lit-
tle-known true account of some of the many thousands of
black soldiers who served on the Union side during the
American Civil War of the 1860s. The war drama focused
on the 54th Regiment of the Massachusetts Voluntary

Infantry. This—the first regiment of black soldiers—was led by a 23-year-old white officer, Robert Gould Shaw (played by Matthew Broderick).

Initially, Denzel had been hesitant to become part of this film project. It was not because he was "reduced" to a supporting role in the cast but rather that he was extremely reluctant to appear in a "slave film." However, after meetings with Zwick and the scenarist, who agreed to flesh out the African-American characters, he accepted. The actor reasoned that this historical combat drama involving ex-slaves was "as a black American, that's my history, and this isn't a [slave story]." As the script was finalized, the story became a study of free men risking their lives to fight for the freedom of all black people in the United States. Since the Caucasian Shaw had been the actual leader of the 54th Regiment, Denzel came to feel more comfortable with a white actor being top-featured in the cast. Once again, he was convinced that participating in this screen venture would help to illuminate to black audiences the brave, little-recorded role that many of their ancestors had played in the Civil War. He further reasoned, "As long as I feel there is an honest portrayal, a fully realized character, then I would do [such a part]."

Shot on location in Massachusetts and Georgia, the $18 million production reached theaters in December 1989. Critical reaction to the movie was mixed, including that of *The New Yorker,* which reported, "*Glory* isn't a great film, but it's a good film on a great subject." However, unlike *Cry Freedom*, which had annoyed many viewers for being a black story told through white eyes, *Glory* evenly balanced its presentation, a situation aided by the exceptionally strong performances offered by the movie's black talent.

As usual, Denzel thoroughly researched his role (including reading old slave journals) as he developed the back story of his runaway slave character. Private Trip is one of the African-American characters (some ex-slaves, others northern farmers, businessmen, and so forth) who willingly risked their lives for the Union cause only to find that they were treated poorly and sometimes cruelly by most of the white Union officers and soldiers. Washington was so in tune with his movie character that he was able sometimes to adlib (make up) dialogue during onscreen moments. Denzel's most heartfelt scene in the picture occurs when his Regiment superiors order him to be whipped for a supposed (and erroneous) infraction of Army rules. As he endures his punishment—the type of treatment that blacks received from their plantation masters in the South—a tear of frustration and resignation trickles down his stern face.

Washington said of this moviemaking experience, "I was happier making *Glory* than I've ever been working on a movie." He attributed this feeling not only to the rare luxury of the cast having a "great deal of rehearsal time" but that he was playing a character that "I really found interesting." He explained further, "He is somebody who makes people uncomfortable, because he's a racist. But he was made a racist by racism. He lived the way he had to live, doing what it took to survive. He wasn't afraid, which I admire."

For his role in Glory, *Denzel earned both an Oscar and a Golden Globe (pictured here) for Best Supporting Actor.* (Photofest)

Glory went on to win several prizes from industry awards competitions. Denzel received many of these prizes. He, like the film, won accolades from the Image Awards given by the National Association for the Advancement of Colored People (NAACP). In addition, Washington claimed a Golden Globe prize as Best Supporting Actor. And, at the Academy Awards in March 1980, Denzel beat out such actor rivals as Marlon Brando and Martin Landau to win the Oscar in the Best Supporting Actor category. On stage at the ceremony, after thanking his wife and mother who were in the audience, he paid homage "to the 54th, the black soldiers who helped to make this country free." After the event, the jubilant Oscar winner told the media, "It's good to be part of the club."

In winning his Oscar, Denzel was only the fifth black performer to ever receive an Academy Award.

Taking a Breather

Denzel felt he needed a lighthearted change of pace after the heavy dramatics of *Glory*. Thus, he next appeared in *Heart Condition* (1990), a comedic fantasy. Washington was cast as suave Napoleon Stone, a lawyer to a drug crowd who is being hounded by a bigoted white cop. The cop suffers a near-fatal heart attack and is rushed to the hospital. There he awakens from surgery to discover that he has a new heart and that the donor's organ came from Stone, who had been fatally shot by an unknown assailant. Thereafter, Napoleon haunts the prejudiced lawman to solve his murder and, when that is accomplished, to encourage the policeman to take good care of his new heart. While the co-stars gave solid performances, the film, with its unlikely and awkward story, found little favorable response from moviegoers.

Enter Spike Lee

When Denzel had appeared off-Broadway in 1981's *When the Chickens Come Home to Roost,* one of the theatergoers impressed by his strong stage performance was future moviemaker Spike Lee. When Washington was on Broadway in 1988's *Checkmates,* Spike saw that play and noted how women in the theater audience responded to Denzel's magnetism. By the 1990s, Lee, who was just in his early thirties, already had a strong reputation within the film industry and with the public as the director of such controversial features as *She's Gotta Have It* (1986) and *Do the Right Thing* (1989). A vocal crusader for Hollywood making more movies about black topics, he was now preparing *Mo' Better Blues* (1990). As was usual with Lee vehicles, the story line would have a current of racial issues underscoring the plot. Spike hired Washington to star in the picture, insisting, "I think this role will free Denzel from playing these great, heroic, stoic types."

To prepare for his assignment as a trumpeter and jazz musician named Bleek Gilliam, Denzel consulted with veteran jazz performer Miles Davis. Washington also studied trumpet with Terence Blanchard (who along with Spike's father, Bill Lee, contributed original music to the film's score). Having learned to play the instrument with sufficient credibility (although much of the music on the soundtrack was dubbed in by Blanchard),

Denzel's work with director Spike Lee (right) in the film
Mo' Better Blues *was the beginning of a long and productive
friendship.* (Photofest)

Denzel began his celluloid role as the self-centered
musician.

Bleek forms his own jazz quartet to play at New
York–area clubs. His rise to success is inhibited by his
near-total self-involvement in his musical career. His

casual attitude toward others extends to his romantic life as he alternates between various love partners, including the two principal women in his life (played by Spike's sister, Joie Lee, and by Cynda Williams).

Lee and Washington developed a good working relationship on the movie set; as a result, Denzel was able to improvise in front of the camera (that is, adding dialogue and actions that aren't in the film's script). However, that bond was disturbed when it came time for Denzel to do his explicitly romantic sequences. Being extremely private by nature and inheriting a degree of conservatism from his preacher father (who died in 1991 at age 81), the actor refused to take off his undershirt—let alone his clothes—for any of the intimate scenes to be filmed. This decision annoyed his two female coleads (who each had to disrobe on-camera) and upset Spike, but Denzel refused to budge on this matter, reasoning that it wasn't proper for a family man to be disrobed on camera.

When released, many reviewers thought the well-acted *Mo' Better Blues* was too ambitious and had not met its creative goals. Many also felt that the picture's underlying racial themes got in the way of the story. In contrast to the picture's mixed reception, Denzel was praised by many sources for providing another engrossing character interpretation. Hal Hinson (*Washington Post*) judged, "Washington gives Bleek a quiet, flashing charm; he delivers a gorgeous, magnetically sexy performance—a true star performance." *Cosmopolitan* magazine decided, "Denzel Washington is a superstar waiting to happen." Made for a cost of $10 million, *Mo' Better Blues* grossed a disappointing $16.2 million in domestic distribution.

Despite the flaws of *Mo' Better Blues*, it was the start of a long-term working relationship between Spike Lee and Denzel Washington.

Meanwhile, with the aid of Denzel's improved salary status in the entertainment business he, Pauletta, and the children had moved to a home in Toluca Lake, an upscale community a few miles northwest of Los Angeles, to accommodate the growing family. To diversify their financial interests, the Washingtons invested in a Los Angeles restaurant named Georgia. In addition, with Flo Allen, a former talent agent, Denzel formed Mundy Lane Entertainment (the name was based on the street where Denzel grew up in Mount Vernon). One of the production company's first projects was *Hank Aaron: Chasing a Dream*, a documentary about baseball that aired on the TBS cable network and eventually claimed an Emmy Award nomination.

A Few Steps Back in His Career

Anxious to get back to his stage acting roots, Denzel was enthusiastic when esteemed stage director Joseph Papp, who had seen Denzel perform in *Checkmates*, asked him to accept the lead role in *Richard III*. This play was to be staged in August 1990 in Central Park as part of the New York Shakespeare Festival.

Playing the lead in this classic drama seemed like a great opportunity for Denzel to reaffirm his live acting talents. However, for some reason, the demanding role of the deformed monarch seemed to elude Washington, whose performance was largely seen as off the mark. John Simon (*New York* magazine) lashed out, "What in his background . . . could have prepared him for a Shakespearian lead?" The trade journal *Backstage* criticized, "The actor's lack of command of the verse doesn't help. The soliloquies [reflective monologues] lose power when Washington runs out of breath by the end of the line or phrase."

In spite of his artistic failure with *Richard III*, Washington told the press, "I'm going to continue to take chances— fall on my face sometimes—but hopefully learn from the experience."

Next, Denzel was scheduled to pair with Michelle Pfeiffer in *Love Field* (1992), an interracial romantic story. However, he withdrew from the project, explaining that his screen character was not sufficiently developed.

Later in 1991 Denzel was again on screen, but this time in a big change of pace from his work in *Cry Freedom* or *Mo' Better Blues*. He starred in a big-budget action picture, the type usually reserved for such white action stars as Sylvester Stallone or Bruce Willis. In *Ricochet,* Denzel played Nick Styles, a Los Angeles police officer who had put a major criminal (played by John Lithgow) behind bars. The latter, a twisted, ingenious individual, eventually

Denzel received unfavorable reviews for his performance in Richard III *in New York's Central Park.* (Photofest)

escapes confinement and sets into motion an elaborate scheme of revenge against Nick, who is now an assistant district attorney. The plot takes many incredible turns, allowing for impressive visual effects and intricate stunt work. For this athletic role, 35-year-old Denzel dieted, exercised, and trained hard. Despite his readiness for the part, the film was not the right showcase for Washington and was a commercial disappointment.

Washington's own reaction to the film was equally negative. About the violent action-film genre, he admitted, "This is not me. I can't do this kind of movie. 'Cause this is mindless violence. I can't be a part of this." On the other hand, the rising star later acknowledged that he constantly encountered fans who ranked *Ricochet* as one of their favorite Denzel movies.

For several years Denzel kept his creative promise to avoid action roles. He returned to the type of small picture in which his talent and personality could shine. For *Mississippi Masala* (1991), a film he fell in love with upon reading the script, he agreed to take far less money than his usual salary so that the project could go forward. Part of the film's title refers to *masala,* an Indian seasoning that blends various-colored spices. This reflects the movie's merging of film genres (comedy, romance, and social ethics) and race in a small Southern town setting. The two lovers in the film are an ambitious African American (played by Denzel) who operates his own carpet-cleaning business and a sheltered young Indian woman (played by Sarita Choudhury) who has immigrated from Uganda. Her family observes the growing relationship between her and the African American with much dismay.

Directed by India's Mira Nair, the low-keyed feature proved to be an uplifting and effective film when released. Peter Travers (*Rolling Stone*) reported, "Washington and newcomer Choudhury are vibrantly expressive as the color-crossed lovers driven apart by racial tensions." The warmhearted, sensitive picture won several prizes at international film festivals. In the United States, for portraying Demetrius Williams, Denzel received an NAACP Image Award in the category of Outstanding Actor in a Motion Picture. For Denzel, this recognition from the NAACP was especially meaningful.

With *Mississippi Masala*, Denzel Washington reaffirmed his acting expertise and charisma. By now, it was becoming an annual event for magazines and polls to name Denzel as one of Hollywood's best-looking and appealing leading men.

5

MALCOLM X

For several years, filmmaker Norman Jewison (director of 1984's *A Soldier's Story,* in which Denzel had performed) had been planning a movie biography of Malcolm X. By the early 1990s Jewison finally had sufficient financing for the film project and had cast Denzel Washington in the demanding title role. This was a dream come true for Denzel, who had wanted to play Malcolm X in film ever since he had portrayed him on stage in the early 1980s.

In the meantime, director Spike Lee had complained to the media about the political incorrectness of Jewison, a white movie director, bringing this major African-American story to the screen. Lee mounted such a strong, continual media protest, that eventually Warner Bros., the producing studio, caved in to his campaign and agreed that he should, instead, direct the feature.

Because Lee himself had long envisioned Denzel in the key role of Malcolm X, he kept Washington as star of his forthcoming picture. However, Lee discarded most of

Jewison's project and started relatively anew. This included throwing out the current screenplay and, instead, using an older script by James Baldwin and Arnold Perl, which was based on *The Autobiography of Malcolm X* (1965) by Malcolm X and Alex Haley.

Heavy-Duty Preparations

To prepare for this major artistic undertaking, Denzel learned as much as he could about Malcolm X. Malcolm X was born in the Midwest in 1925 as Malcolm Little. As a youngster he and his family had suffered racial discrimination and endured poverty. The boy had experienced his Baptist-minister father being murdered by the Ku Klux Klan. As a young man, Malcolm moved to Harlem and became a small-time burglar. Thereafter he had gone to Boston (where he had lived before) to further pursue his life of petty crime. Eventually he was arrested and sentenced to years behind bars. During his lengthy prison stay, he gained spirituality and a new philosophical/political perspective by studying the preaching of the Nation of Islam. He then renamed himself Malcolm X.

When he was released from prison in 1952, he became an active spokesperson for the Nation of Islam, guided by that group's Elijah Muhammad (played in the film by Al Freeman Jr.). Later, Malcolm X wed Betty Shabazz (played

Portraying Malcolm X on film was like a dream come true for Denzel. (Photofest)

by Angela Bassett), a Muslim nurse, and carried on his preaching against the white race. As Malcolm X grew in influence, he incurred the suspicion of Elijah Muhammad. In 1964, Malcolm X abandoned the Nation of Islam and embarked on a pilgrimage to Mecca (in western Saudi Arabia), the birthplace of Muhammad. Proclaiming himself to be El-Hajj Malik El-Shabazz, the rededicated leader returned to America. By now he had discarded his belief in racial separation, having become a firm believer in the eventual unification of blacks and whites. In February 1965, at age 39, Malcolm X was assassinated in a Harlem ballroom, purportedly killed by followers of the Nation of Islam.

With location filming in New York, Massachusetts, Connecticut, Egypt, Saudi Arabia, and South Africa, the elaborate, 202-minute *Malcolm X* cost $32 million to make. As Denzel explained to film critic Roger Ebert, "This was the first film where I did not want to stop shooting, especially the speeches. Once I got used to it, I just kept going and going." Washington also recalled, "Throughout the film I lived Malcolm's life whether the cameras were on or off." The movie star revealed, "The hardest scene for me to shoot was probably the assassination. There was a dark feeling on the set, and I felt shackled in it. . . . The first take that we did, we had to stop, and some people were crying and upset. It was an emotional couple of days."

With humility, Denzel told Ebert, "I can't be Malcolm X. I'm not Malcolm X. But I think I can motivate or inspire — be a tool, hopefully, to do some good in this world." In terms of working again with Spike Lee, Washington acknowledged, "Spike's not an actor's director. Coming to this film I knew what to expect, so it was real smooth. Spike was more open to my ideas on this one, more collaborative." Summing up his memorable experience (which encompassed over a year and a half of work), Denzel said, "Everything I have done as an actor has been in preparation for this."

By the time that *Malcolm X* was shown in theaters in mid-November 1992, the highly controversial movie had been so hyped (and merchandised with tie-in products such as baseball caps and T-shirts) that it would have been practically impossible to meet critics and audiences' expectations. *Daily Variety* pointed out, "The picture comes up short in several departments, notably in pacing and in giving a strong sense of why this man became a legend." As to the film's lead actor, Vincent Canby (*New York Times*) endorsed, "Mr. Washington not only looks the part, but he also has the psychological heft, the intelligence and the reserve to give the film the dramatic excitement that isn't always apparent in the screenplay." The *Los Angeles Times* judged, "Washington's Malcolm is a heroic performance in several senses, calling for him to be on screen in almost every scene and to make all those transformations believable, and the actor does it all with a special grace."

Malcolm X was not the booming box-office hit many people had anticipated. The film claimed only two Oscar nominations: Best Actor and Best Costumes. Denzel lost in his category to Al Pacino, but insisted in a *Gentlemen's Quarterly* interview in January 1994, "I didn't lose any sleep before or after. It sounds like a stock answer, but it's the truth." Washington, however, did win, among others, a New York Film Critics Circle Award and an MTV Movie Awards trophy for

Best Male Performance. At the 26th Annual NAACP Image Awards, Denzel received Outstanding Actor in a Motion Picture prize for his *Malcolm X* performance.

Changes of Pace

After his emotionally draining work on *Malcolm X*, Denzel accepted an offer to play Don Pedro, the prince of Aragon and the half-brother of Don John (played by Keanu Reeves), in the Shakespearean comedy *Much Ado About Nothing* (1993). Washington took this supporting assignment because he wanted to work with director/star Kenneth Branagh and he welcomed another opportunity to test his skills in a Shakespearean work, especially after his faltering stage performance in 1990's *Richard III*. Wearing a moustache and trimmed beard for this production, Denzel was rated "subdued but graceful" (*Sight and Sound* magazine). Within weeks of this film's release, Denzel was the new recipient of the Spencer Tracy Award from UCLA for his overall body of acting work.

That same year Julia Roberts, the queen of the Hollywood box-office, returned to moviemaking after a two-year vacation. She starred in *The Pelican Brief*, a thriller based on John Grisham's best-selling novel of the same name. To the surprise of many industry onlookers, Roberts wanted Denzel to be hired to play her leading man—that of the Washington, D.C., investigative reporter who comes to her rescue when she uncovers a deadly political conspiracy. Although Grisham's original book had presented the character of Gray Grantham as a white journalist—one who falls in love with the law-student heroine—the Warner Bros. film does not include the romantic subplot. The film's creators insisted that this change was not made out of concern about showing an interracial romance but because such a relationship would detract from the thriller.

Entertainment Weekly ranked *The Pelican Brief* a "C–" explaining that the movie "settles into a deadening rhythm of snoop, get chased, hide in a hotel room, snoop, get chased, hide in a hotel room." But the same reviewer said that Roberts and Washington did their best with the poor script. As to Washington's performance, Roger Ebert (*Chicago Sun-Times*) cited, he "shows again how credible he seems on the screen; like Spencer Tracy, he can make you believe in almost any character." *Time* magazine concurred: "Washington underplays suavely, it's almost impossible to muffle his charisma." *The Pelican Brief* was a profitable crossover into mainstream cinema for Denzel after the highly political *Malcolm X.*

Another Blockbuster

Within days of the release of *The Pelican Brief,* Denzel appeared on screen in another major production,

Philadelphia (1993). Unlike the commercial thriller *The Pelican Brief, Philadelphia* was a decidedly controversial drama. It was a major studio movie about the enormously sensitive topics of discrimination against homosexuals and AIDS victims.

The film stars Tom Hanks as a successful Pennsylvania attorney at a wealthy corporate law firm who is suddenly fired from his post. Hanks's character suspects that his dismissal was not for his legal work but because his employers had discovered that he was suffering from AIDS. Although he is determined to fight back, Hanks's character has great difficulty finding a lawyer to represent him in his lawsuit. Finally, Joe Miller (played by Denzel), a small-time attorney and family man who is homophobic, accepts the challenge and battles the odds in the courtroom to prove his dying client's difficult case. In the process, Miller gains an understanding and respect for his client, homosexuals, and the reality of AIDS.

As in *The Pelican Brief,* Washington's part was originally conceived for a white performer and his role was subordinate to his colead. The experience of burrowing into his bigoted character gave Denzel an opportunity to examine the issues of homophobia and paranoia about AIDS victims. At the end of his enlightening participation in this film, Denzel said, "I don't think I am anything like . . .

[my] character . . . but I think I got a chance to vent certain frustrations, maybe. It was a good education."

Denzel earned good reviews for his performance in *Philadelphia*. The *Los Angeles Times* enthused, "It was once thought an almost scientific impossibility that Washington could top his [*Malcolm X*] performance . . . but [in *Philadelphia*] he seems to redefine intensity and passion." The *Hollywood Reporter* labeled Denzel "engagingly scrappy." *People* magazine argued, "Washington provides strong support," and *Daily Variety* judged him

Tom Hanks and Denzel in Philadelphia *(Photofest)*

"first-rate as the attorney dragged reluctantly out of his own selfishness."

Thanks to two back-to-back box-office megahits, it was little wonder that Denzel Washington was now commanding an $8 million salary per film. His fee was rising due to his unique appeal to a wide range of moviegoers, no matter what their racial and economical background.

With his remarkable industry success, Washington was much in demand for media interviews. However, he still refused to discuss his personal life. He did say that he got a great deal of satisfaction out of being a family man who was responsive to his children's needs, whether at home, at school, at church, or on the sports playing field (where Denzel often served as coach for his children's teams). He and wife Pauletta took advantage of their growing financial good fortune to increase their charitable donations and to participate in causes close to their heart—especially those related to helping the black community, AIDS victims, and disadvantaged children.

Back into Action

A few years earlier, after the failure of 1991's *Ricochet*, Denzel had vowed not to star in any more action movies. However, he had a change of heart when his son begged his dad to stop making "old-folks movies" and "do some action movies." Taking the request seriously, the movie star complied over the next few years.

Crimson Tide (1995) gave Denzel an opportunity to work again with Gene Hackman (with whom he had appeared in *Power*). In this thriller, Russian rebels have taken over a long-range missile base in the former USSR. In response, the United States dispatches a nuclear submarine (the USS *Alabama*) to be on hand to retaliate in case the Russian base attacks America. During this highly charged situation, the vessel receives a message from higher-ups but can only decipher part of the command because its radio system has been damaged by enemy activity. Hackman's captain and Washington's lieutenant commander have different opinions as to their next course of action. It leads to various mutinies aboard the *Alabama* and a fight for control of the submarine's deadly nuclear missiles.

Mick LaSalle (*San Francisco Chronicle*) lauded this summer film: "[It] has everything you could want from an action thriller and a few other things you usually can't hope to expect: an excellent script, first-rate performances and a story that has more to do with individuals than explosions." He further praised, "Washington has always been an appealing star, but in *Crimson Tide* we find him, in this leading man role, more convincing than ever." The film was a box-office hit, and Denzel received another

NAACP Image Award for Outstanding Actor in a Motion Picture for this role.

Paramount's *Virtuosity* (1995), a sci-fi thriller that tapped the growing public interest in computers, the Internet, and cyberspace, was released a few months later. In this film Denzel plays a cop with a twisted past who is paroled from prison to fight a virtual-reality serial killer. The special effects–laden feature was unable to generate audience interest. Reflecting on this unsuccessful venture, Denzel observed that it was "one of the hardest films I've ever done" and that "You gotta run and jump and you don't talk. It's not acting."

Assessing the situation, Washington determined to return to the type of filmmaking he knew best—stories that were character-driven and did not revolve around high-blown special effects.

6

THE BOX-OFFICE WINNER

After several years of preparation, in 1995 Denzel felt ready to produce a full-length feature film for the Mundy Lane Entertainment company that he had formed back in 1990.

For his first production effort, he chose to bring the dark tale *Devil in a Blue Dress* to the screen. Based on Walter Mosley's 1990 novel and directed by Carl Franklin, it was one of several books featuring African-American private eye Ezikeal "Easy" Rawlins and set in Los Angeles (in the 1940s and thereafter). Producer/star Denzel plays Rawlins, a World War II veteran, unemployed aircraft-factory worker, and private eye. He is hired to locate a missing white woman (played by Jennifer Beals) thought to be in hiding in South Central, the city's black neighborhood.

In the process, he meets a wide variety of eccentric and often dangerous characters.

Hal Hinson (*Washington Post*) said of *Devil in a Blue Dress,* "The film's principal virtue, is its sense of reality—in particular the reality of segregated Los Angeles in the '40s." Peter Travers (*Rolling Stone*) praised Denzel's "richly detailed portrayal" of Easy.

Despite the movie's many virtues—which included the realistic period atmosphere and the exploration of serious racial issues—many felt the plot was too complicated. Also, movie audiences who expected a sizzling romance between Denzel's and Beals's characters, as had been the case in the book original, were sadly disappointed. Overall, the film was a commercial misstep.

Having made several back-to-back films, an exhausted Denzel fulfilled a promise he made when shooting *Cry Freedom* a few years earlier. He took his family on a safari to Africa. They visited Tanzania, Kenya, the island of Zanzibar, and, later, made a stopover in South Africa. By then apartheid had ended in South Africa and the country's distinguished president, Nelson Mandela, was on hand to greet Denzel and his family. While in South Africa, Washington and Pauletta renewed their wedding vows in a ceremony conducted by Archbishop Desmond Tutu, the country's chief religious leader.

In Top Form

Refreshed and in top acting form after his trip abroad, Denzel reunited with director Edward Zwick (*Glory*) for the big-budget 20th Century Fox release *Courage under Fire* (1996). Washington beat out Tom Hanks and Harrison Ford to gain this role, and, as his prize, claimed a $10 million salary. Co-starring Meg Ryan and Lou Diamond Phillips, this was the first major studio film to deal with the 1991 Gulf War. Denzel is seen as Lieutenant Colonel Nathaniel Sterling who is ordered to decide whether the deceased Captain Emma Walden (Ryan), a medevac pilot, should receive the Medal of Honor for bravery in the line of fire. Before the honor can be bestowed—the first such given to a woman—Sterling must interview Walden's surviving crew, each of whom has a different take on what actually happened during the fateful mission. Clouding his investigation is his guilt and grief over members of his tank unit who had recently died.

Ever the professional, Denzel researched his role by observing closely a tank group at the Army's National Training Center at Fort Irwin in Northern California. His preparation included participating in tank artillery maneuvers and complex battle simulations. Impressed by his experiences on the base and in field maneuvers, the star observed, "The one thing I kept finding out about these men and women is that they're not just cardboard

Rambos." He also noted, "The research I did made me understand the importance of integrity."

Released during the summer blockbuster season, *Courage under Fire* had a lot of competition for moviegoers' attention. Reviews of the film, including Denzel's performance in it, were mixed. However, Denzel received yet another NAACP Image Award for Outstanding Actor in a Motion Picture, and he was also named NAACP Entertainer of the Year.

Teaming with Whitney Houston

In 1996, Denzel co-starred with pop diva Whitney Houston in *The Preacher's Wife,* a remake of the 1947 film *The Bishop's Wife*. In this film directed by Penny Marshall, Denzel plays an angel named Dudley, who is sent to Earth to help Reverend Henry Biggs with professional difficulties and his troubled marriage to Julia (Houston), the congregation's choir director. Dudley charms Julia and wins over the confidence of her young son. But he has more trouble restoring Henry's faith and helping him through his many dilemmas.

For Denzel, *The Preacher's Wife* was a refreshing change of pace; for a rare occasion, he was not playing a brooding, dramatic role. He reasoned, "I've done films with the edge, drama, weight, and all that. I just thought we had an excellent opportunity to talk about faith and family."

With its stirring gospel score and many musical numbers performed by Houston and the impressive Georgia Mass Choir, there were high expectations for *The Preacher's Wife*. However, the critical consensus was that the good-hearted picture was too sweet and sentimental and that its pacing often dragged. Also, there seemed to be an essential lack of chemistry between Denzel and Whitney, and some said Denzel did not provide quite the right light touch in his performance.

One role Denzel vetoed in this period was 1997's *Amistad*, a big-budget tale of mutinous slaves in 19th-century America. Washington said he turned down the lucrative assignment because, "I ain't putting no chains around my neck. I'm not in the mood."

Instead, Denzel moved on to a trio of features released in 1998. First was the horror thriller *Fallen*. This film cast Washington again as a police detective in pursuit of a serial killer. Filled with endless plot complications, this dark film about good forces versus evil demons was not well received by critics or viewers.

After *Fallen*, Denzel turned to 1998's *He Got Game,* his third film with Spike Lee. In this drama written, directed, and produced by Lee, Washington took a supporting role. This film's star was Rae Allen, a real-life basketball star who plays Denzel's on-screen son. The film tells the story of a hugely talented high-school basketball champ, his imprisoned father, and both of their plans for the son's future. The earnest film was not a major crowd pleaser. However, for *He Got Game*, Denzel was nominated in the Best Actor category at the Acapulco Black Film Festival and by the NAACP Image Awards, but lost on both occasions. Regardless of the picture's financial and artistic outcome, Washington found the film's dramatic themes stimulating. He also enjoyed the opportunity to play basketball on camera.

Another Go at the Action Genre

Denzel was matched yet again with filmmaker Edward Zwick for 20th Century Fox's *The Siege* (1998). Denzel shared screen time with Bruce Willis and Annette Bening in this terrorist tale set in New York City.

Of more substance was *The Bone Collector* (1999), a cop-versus–serial killer film with a twist. This plot gimmick provided Denzel with a major acting challenge. His character, Lincoln Rhyme, a superior New York police detective and forensic expert, has suffered an on-the-job accident. He is now a quadriplegic, suffering from paralysis of his body below the neck. Extremely depressed by his plight, Rhyme contemplates suicide, but his spirits are renewed when he helps a female investigator (Angelina Jolie) solve a crime from the confines of his apartment.

The artistic challenge for Washington was to make his quadriplegic character—who only has the use of one index finger—believable and dimensional. As part of building his character, Denzel contacted actor Christopher Reeve (star of the film *Superman* who became a quadriplegic) for advice on performing this offbeat role. Although many critics said the acting surpassed the film's tired plot lines, *The Bone Collector* did well in theaters and enabled Denzel to tackle new acting challenges.

A Renewed Commitment

As the 1990s ended, Denzel took stock of his career. All of his films since 1996's *Courage under Fire* had received mixed critical response and had not done stellar box-office business. Mindful that, as a high-profile movie star earning more than $10 million for each of his big-budget vehicles, he could quickly lose credibility with critics and public alike, he decided to balance his film output with more substantial vehicles. Now in his mid-40s, the popular Hollywood leading man told *Premiere* magazine in December 1999, "Anything that I do now, it's got to be something that I want to do 100 percent." He also reflected, "This is an important and interesting time for me." He emphasized his point when he said, "I've gone all the way around the block [with acting assignments], and I've gotten back to the work."

7

MAINTAINING THE PACE

For Denzel, constantly finding new professional challenges and not becoming lazy from success were his most imperative career guidelines. Fortunately, his next motion picture would meet all his creative needs and moviegoers' expectations . . . and then some.

The Hurricane

After tackling less-than-substantial film projects, Denzel realized the career importance of his upcoming film role in Universal's *The Hurricane* (1999). For the part, Washington spent 15 months in heavy-duty training: He had to lose more than 40 pounds and endure daily workouts for his physically demanding role of Rubin "Hurricane" Carter, a middleweight boxing champ.

Washington worked diligently with a boxing trainer—former fight champ Terry Claybon—so that he would look believable on camera in the boxing scenes. Denzel reasoned, if the audience "don't buy that, you're done." By the time filming began for *The Hurricane*, Denzel was in the best physical shape of his life.

Working again with Norman Jewison (*A Soldier's Story*), Denzel portrays a real-life professional fighter who finds himself in prison for crimes he insists he did not commit. After Hurricane spends years in prison, a fifteen-year old in Toronto becomes convinced of Hurricane's innocence and persuades his foster family to help him fight for the

Denzel lost more than 40 pounds and underwent intense workouts for his role in The Hurricane. *(Photofest)*

boxer's release. After many setbacks, a federal court judge in 1985 voids the athlete's convictions as being unconstitutional, and Hurricane is freed.

Stephen Holden (*New York Times*) was far more impressed with Denzel's compelling lead performance than with the film as a whole: "Washington leans into an otherwise schlocky movie and slams it out of the ballpark. If his Hurricane is an inspiring portrait of nobility, it is because the actor never conceals the demons of fury and despair gnawing beneath his character's forcefully articulate surface."

Made for $38 million, *The Hurricane* took in $50.7 million in domestic distribution. Denzel received an Academy Award nomination for Best Actor for the role. However, media articles appeared that criticized the screen biography for being a highly fictionalized, abbreviated account of the legal injustice in Rubin Carter's conviction and the real part that racial prejudice had played in the man's fate. The controversy over the film's portrayal of these issues—none of which altered the fact that the man had been wrongly sent to prison—became a distracting issue in the minds of many viewers. Some observers insist this was a key reason why Denzel lost the Oscar that year. Washington, however, did win, among other prizes, a Golden Globe and an NAACP Image Award.

Another Sports Film

Moving on to a less controversial film assignment, Denzel next starred in Walt Disney Pictures' *Remember the Titans* (2000). Based on a true story, the film is set in 1971 in Alexandria, Virginia, where federal law had ordered that a local high school be racially integrated. As part of the revamped school system, Herman Boone (played by Washington) is selected to be head coach over his white counterpart, which causes a tidal wave of local resentment. During the difficult year ahead, Denzel's no-nonsense but compassionate character deals—both at school and in the community—with racial tension as the townsfolk cope with an integrated way of daily life. However, as Washington's football squad of black and white students learns to work in harmony, the locals begin to abandon some of their discriminatory ways.

Many critics claimed that *Remember the Titans* was too sentimental, but many praised Denzel's performance. Mick LaSalle (*San Francisco Chronicle*) noted, "As played by Washington, Boone is more than tough. He is a man of keen observation and restraint, and some of the film's best moments provide a glimpse into his inner world."

Washington so believed in this inspirational project that he took a pay cut so that *Remember the Titans* could be made within its $30 million budget. Having coached his youngsters' sports teams over the years, the star felt comfortable in his role of Coach Boone who gains insight into his own life by motivating his high-spirited team. For his heartfelt performance, Denzel won in the Best Actor category from the Black Entertainment Awards, the Black Reel Awards, and the NAACP Image Awards.

Claiming Another Oscar

Over his lengthy screen career Denzel had most frequently been cast as the well-meaning, noble soul. This was definitely not the case with his role in *Training Day* (2001), a gripping Warner Bros. crime thriller. While Washington again appeared as a police officer, this time he was a corrupt undercover narcotics cop. To highlight this change-of-pace acting assignment for filmgoers, Denzel's Alonzo Harris is outfitted in black, wears thick jewelry, and sports a tattoo which contains his creed for life: DEATH IS CERTAIN. LIFE IS NOT.

The hard-hitting, brutal film follows Alonzo through a wild day in his life as part of an elite Los Angeles police unit. He is joined by a white rookie cop (played by Ethan Hawke) who is a candidate to join Harris's special group of law enforcers. As the duo make their rounds, the newcomer concludes that Alonzo may well be as vicious and crooked as the ferocious lawbreakers they are hunting. Eventually, Alonzo's bad karma catches up with him as he seeks to outmaneuver Russian mobsters.

Ethan Hawke and Denzel in Training Day (Photofest)

Whatever faults critics found with *Training Day*, there was strong appreciation for Denzel's intense performance. Roger Ebert (*Chicago Sun-Times*) admitted, "For its kinetic energy and acting zeal, I enjoyed the movie. I like it when actors go for broke." Kim Newman (*Sight and Sound*) applauded Washington's "spellbinding villain," Amy Taubin (*Village Voice*) pointed out, "Actors always have more fun playing bad guys—and in Washington's case, it must be particularly liberating not to bear the weight of being a black role model. . . . You have to admire the risk he takes in turning his star image upside down; nevertheless, it's creepy to think that the hero you believed in for so many movies may be just as much a fiction as the villain."

Shot on location in the grimier parts of Los Angeles, Washington took on this atypical role with great enthusiasm. He became so in tune with his alter ego that he improvised much of his fast-paced dialogue as he led the young cop (and the audience) through a shocking tour of the criminal underworld. As a way to constantly keep himself in the mindset of his offbeat character, the actor scribbled a note to himself in his script: "The wages of sin [are] death." These words, he later recalled, helped him a great deal with his distinctive performance: "Every time I looked at those words, I felt like I could be as wicked as I wanted to be because I know what was coming [for my character]." When asked why he had taken on this unusual part, he explained, "I think it's good to get a bad guy in there to mix up my image."

Training Day proved to be a medium box-office winner but a critical favorite. Besides earning his second Academy Award—his first in the Best Actor category—Washington won trophies from several film critics groups, as well as the NAACP Image Award. At the MTV Awards, Denzel was named Best Villain of the Year.

Denzel as Everyman

Having proved his point that he could be more versatile on screen than his good-guy roles had previously allowed,

Denzel returned to form in *John Q* (2002). The film is an impassioned account about the need for health-care reform, a subject with which Denzel greatly empathized. The New Line Cinema release is about a Chicago factory worker who is a devoted husband and father. When his nine-year-old son suffers a seizure, John Quincy Archibald (played by Denzel) discovers that, because he does not have sufficient health-care coverage, his boy cannot have a needed emergency heart transplant. Desperate to save his boy's life, and having exhausted all options to raise the needed funds, Washington's character takes the hospital's chief cardiac surgeon hostage and demands that his dying child be placed on the donor recipient list. Not yielding to the pressures of the police negotiator and the law enforcers surrounding the facility—or to the media frenzy that has developed over the situation—Archibald stays firm in his goal.

Claudia Puig (*USA Today*) related well to the movie's premise: "If you're privileged, you'll get the medical help you need, but that's not the case for the common man." As for the star, she judged, "It's a testament to his talents that the movie doesn't lapse into an *ER*-like, tear-inducing episode. Washington's character is the ultimate super-dad—a manipulative device—but we would have been rooting for him anyway." This review suggested that, by now, audiences of any race or economic standing were more than willing to identify with the characters whom Denzel played.

Reaching Out Artistically

Many established film actors—ranging from Sidney Poitier to Clint Eastwood to Mel Gibson—reach the point in their acting careers when they feel the need for fresh creative stimulus. Often, they turn to directing a movie as a new artistic challenge. In Denzel Washington's case, he chose to direct *Antwone Fisher* (2002).

His production company, Mundy Lane Entertainment, in conjunction with 20th Century Fox, made this real-life drama derived from Antwone Fisher's book (*Finding Fish*) and screenplay. The movie concerns a young U.S. Navy ensign who has violently attacked people without provocation. His superior officers send him for counseling with a Navy psychiatrist (Washington). The therapist delves into his patient's childhood and the traumatic events that occurred then, pushing the young man to confront his repressed memories. This process helps not only the patient, but it enables the psychiatrist to work through domestic issues in his own marriage.

Denzel's directorial debut was generally well received. Ann Hornaday (*Washington Post*) said, "The directorial debut of Denzel Washington . . . is a piece of controlled, adroit film-making, as notable for what it doesn't do as for what it does

Denzel was behind the camera as director for the first time in Antwone Fisher. *(Photofest)*

so well. . . . Washington ensures that what could have been a mawkish melodrama is instead a riveting story well told." Roger Ebert (*Chicago Sun-Times*) approved that the on-screen "relationship between the two men is handled by Washington, as the director, with close and caring attention." Stephen Holden (*New York Times*) assessed, "As a director Mr. Washington shows a confident grasp of cinematic narrative in a hearty meat-and-potatoes style. But the most remarkable aspect of his behind-the-camera debut is his brilliantly surefooted handling of actors."

Antwone Fisher won several nominations and awards, especially for its young lead's breakthrough performance. Denzel took home three NAACP Image Awards for his work in 2002: one for his role in *John Q* and one each for starring in and directing *Antwone Fisher*, which was named outstanding motion picture. For Denzel, this film-making experience proved that his talents extended behind the camera, and he has indicated that he will direct other features in the years to come, but he would prefer next time not to direct himself. He found that too distracting on *Antwone Fisher*.

Keeping in the Game

Meanwhile, to balance his directorial endeavors, Denzel returned to being a leading man in MGM's *Out of Time* (2003), working again with director Carl Franklin (*Devil in*

In 2003, Denzel received three NAACP Image Awards for his acting and directorial efforts. (Landov)

a Blue Dress). The entry updated the classic 1948 film noir *The Big Clock*. Set in small-town Florida where Washington's Matt Lee Whitlock is police chief, the plot shifts into gear when the lawman steals drug money to pay for his mistress's experimental cancer treatment. Later, he finds himself accused of murdering the woman and her husband, especially since he was named her beneficiary in a large insurance policy. To make matters more complex, the policeman's estranged wife is investigating the case.

Elvis Mitchell (*New York Times*) found the film "shallow" and "empty." However, the reviewer acknowledged that the star plays "the desperation well." Michael Wilmington (*Chicago Tribune*) reported, "Washington is a good center for this type of movie. He's able to simultaneously project intelligence, strength and vulnerability while also revealing the devilish streak that took over *Training Day*." Wilmington also pointed out, "He can get a cunning, menacing edge that makes him a model bad guy. That helps his performance here, and it also helps that he's a black police chief in a white town, with a white sidekick, because he's able to play a natural outsider, seemingly both menacing and menaced."

Shot on location in Florida, the $50 million thriller was not the commercial success anticipated, but Denzel was praised for once again being able to work with some of the darker qualities he exhibited in *Training Day*.

Looking Ahead

Approaching age 50, Denzel continued onward with his lucrative career as an A-list film star. In *Man on Fire* (2004), he was cast as an ex-special forces soldier who vows vengeance on those who kidnapped the little girl he was hired to protect. For Paramount's *The Manchurian Candidate* (2004), Washington inherited Frank Sinatra's original role as the investigating hero of U.S. soldiers who are kidnapped and brainwashed during (in the updated version) the Gulf War.

In assessing Denzel's role as a long-term box-office magnet, Alan J. Pakula, who directed 1993's *The Pelican Brief,* once said, "A lot of actors need to prove something. I don't feel that with Denzel. He doesn't have that torture, that self-doubt you find in some actors. Maybe it's a sense of self-belief." It is also that the star has a realistic attitude about each movie he makes, no matter how much energy, hard work, and emotion he may have invested in the part. He reasons that making a film is "just like a muffin. You make it. You put it on the table. One person might say, 'Oh, I don't like it.' One might say it's the best muffin ever made. One might say it's an awful muffin. It's hard for me to say. It's for me to make the muffin."

Washington, who remains very family oriented, admits that his years of marriage and parenting have improved

Denzel and his wife, Pauletta Washington (Landov)

his acting skills. He says, "I think that fatherhood has loosened me up. I think I've always been funny. It has to do with the way I trained as an actor. I started off, I cut my teeth on *Othello* and Eugene O'Neill and Strindberg and *A Soldier's Play*, that's what I became because that's what I did. When someone in your youth calls you a 'serious actor,' you say, 'Yes, I am.' As you get older, you learn how to simply live your life. I used to be more brooding. I think, than I am now." He also maintains, "Whatever gifts I have been given, I work from the inside out, not from the outside in. I'm not a look. I'm an actor." He also emphasizes, "I enjoy acting—this is when I feel more natural. This is really my world."

Denzel still maintains that he is not a black role model, but, rather, that he wants to be considered a professional actor who has helped to break down racial barriers. He insists that years of praise have not gone to his head: "I try to be ego-less, if there is such a thing. I try to stay humble and hungry . . . just hungry to be good at my job. A little hunger is good for you."

Once, when asked what epitaph he would like on his tombstone, the superstar said, "Hard work is good enough."

TIME LINE

1954   Born in Mount Vernon, New York, on December 28, the second of three children

1968   Parents divorce; Denzel attends Oakland Academy in New Windsor, New York

1972   Graduates from Oakland Academy; enrolls at Fordham University, where he leaves during sophomore year but returns to complete his education, majoring in journalism and drama

1977   Has first professional acting role, in TV movie *Wilma* (NBC-TV), during the production of which he meets actress/musician Pauletta Pearson; graduates from Fordham; relocates to San Francisco to study at the American Conservatory Theater (ACT)

1978   Drops out of ACT; after a brief stay in Los Angeles to search for a job, returns to New York where he is cast in several off-Broadway theater productions

1979   Featured in the television film *Flesh and Blood* (CBS-TV)

1981   Stars off-Broadway as Malcolm X in *When the Chickens Come Home to Roost* and wins an Audelco Award; earns an Obie Award for his performance in *A Soldier's Play*; co-stars in first theatrical feature film, *Carbon Copy* (Avco-Embassy)

1982   Begins six-season run as Dr. Phillip Chandler on TV series *St. Elsewhere* (NBC-TV)

1983   Weds Pauletta Pearson

1984   Co-stars in TV movie *License to Kill* (CBS-TV) and feature film *A Soldier's Story* (Columbia); son John David born

1986   Has title role in television feature *The George McKenna Story* (CBS-TV) and is featured in the film *Power* (20th Century Fox)

1987   Nominated for an Academy Award for Best Supporting Actor in *Cry Freedom* (Universal)

1988   Stars in *For Queen and Country* (Atlantic Releasing); daughter Katia is born

1989   Has leading role in *The Mighty Quinn* (MGM); wins Academy Award, Golden Globe, and NAACP Image Award for his supporting role in *Glory* (TriStar)

1990 Appears in *Heart Condition* (New Line Cinema) and in Spike Lee's *Mo' Better Blues* (Universal); forms Mundy Lane Entertainment production company

1991 *Mississippi Masala* (Samuel Goldwyn) and *Ricochet* (Warner Bros.) are released; twins Malcolm and Olivia are born; Denzel's father dies

1992 Nominated for an Academy Award and Golden Globe for *Malcolm X* (Warner Bros.); wins several prizes for Best Actor including the NAACP Image Award, the Berlin Film Festival Silver Bear Award, and the MTV Movie Award

1993 *Much Ado About Nothing* (Samuel Goldwyn), *The Pelican Brief* (Warner Bros.), and *Philadelphia* (TriStar) are released

1995 For *Crimson Tide* (Hollywood) Denzel receives an NAACP Image Award for Outstanding Actor; stars in *Virtuosity* (Paramount); stars/produces *Devil in a Blue Dress* (TriStar)

1996 For *Courage under Fire* (20th Century Fox) earns a NAACP Image Award for Outstanding Actor; stars/produces *The Preacher's Wife* (Touchstone)

1998 *Fallen* (Warner Bros.), *He Got Game* (Touchstone), and *Siege* (20th Century Fox) are released; named one of top 10 most popular film stars by the Harris Poll

1999 *The Bone Collector* (Columbia/Universal) appears; for *The Hurricane* (Universal) he is nominated for a Best Actor Academy Award and wins a Golden Globe and an NAACP Image Award

2000 *Remember the Titans* (Walt Disney) distributed; wins an NAACP Image Award

2001 *Training Day* (Warner Bros) released, which leads to Best Actor Academy Award, an NAACP Image Award, and other accolades

2002 Stars in *John Q* (New Line Cinema); makes feature film directing debut with *Antwone Fisher* (20th Century Fox)

2003 *Out of Time* (MGM) distributed; wins three NAACP Image Awards for his role in *John Q* and for starring in and directing *Antwone Fisher*

2004 Stars in *Man on Fire* (20th Century Fox) and *The Manchurian Candidate* (Paramount); in production to star in *The Blue* (Universal), a comedy/thriller, and is scheduled to direct *The Great Debaters*, as well as produce/direct a screen biography of the late entertainer Sammy Davis Jr.

HOW TO BECOME AN ACTOR

THE JOB

The imitation or basic development of a character for presentation to an audience may seem like a glamorous and fairly easy job. In reality, it is demanding, tiring work that requires a special talent.

An actor must first find an available part in an upcoming production. This may be in a comedy, drama, musical, or opera. Then, having read and studied the part, the actor must audition before the director and other people who have control of the production. This requirement is often waived for established artists. In film and television, actors must also complete screen tests, which are scenes recorded on film, at times performed with other actors, which are later viewed by the director and producer(s) of the film.

If selected for the part, the actor must spend hundreds of hours in rehearsal and must memorize many lines and cues. This is especially true in live theater; in film and television actors may spend less time in rehearsal and sometimes improvise their lines before the camera, often performing several attempts, or "takes," before the director is satisfied. Television actors often take advantage of TelePrompTers, which scroll lines on a screen in front of performing actors. Radio actors generally read from a script, and therefore their rehearsal times are usually shorter.

In addition to such mechanical duties, the actor must determine the essence of the character he or she is auditioning for, and the relation of that character to the overall scheme of the production. Radio actors must be especially skilled in expressing character and emotion through voice alone. In many film and theater roles actors must also sing and dance and spend additional time rehearsing songs and perfecting choreography. Certain roles require actors to perform various stunts, some of which can be quite dangerous. Specially trained performers usually complete these stunts. Others work as stand-ins or body doubles. These actors are chosen for specific features and appear on film in place of the lead actor;

this is often the case in films requiring nude or seminude scenes. Many television programs, such as game shows, also feature models, who generally assist the host of the program.

Actors in the theater may perform the same part many times a week for weeks, months, and sometimes years. This allows them to develop the role, but it can also become tedious. Actors in films may spend several weeks involved in a production, which often takes place on location (that is, in different parts of the world). Television actors involved in a series, such as a soap opera or a situation comedy, also may play the same role for years, generally in 13-week cycles. For these actors, however, their lines change from week to week and even from day to day, and much time is spent rehearsing their new lines.

While studying and perfecting their craft, many actors work as extras, the nonspeaking characters who appear in the background on screen or stage. Many actors also continue training throughout their careers. A great deal of an actor's time is spent attending auditions.

REQUIREMENTS
High School
There are no minimum educational requirements to become an actor. However, at least a high school diploma is recommended. In high-school English classes you will

learn about the history of drama and the development of strong characters. Take music classes to help you develop your voice and ability to read music, which are valuable skills for any actor, even those who do not perform many musical roles.

Postsecondary Training

A college degree is becoming a great asset to those who hope to have an acting career. An actor who has completed a liberal arts program is thought to be more capable of understanding the wide variety of roles that are available. Therefore, it is strongly recommended that aspiring actors complete at least a bachelor's degree program in theater or the dramatic arts. In addition, graduate degrees in the fine arts or in drama are nearly always required should the individual decide to teach dramatic arts.

College can also provide acting experience for the hopeful actor. More than 500 colleges and universities throughout the country offer dramatic-arts programs and present theatrical performances. Actors and directors recommend that those students interested in acting gain as much experience as possible through acting in high school and college plays or in those offered by community groups. Training beyond college is recommended, especially for actors interested in entering the theater. Joining acting workshops, such as the Actors Studio, can often be highly competitive.

Other Requirements

Prospective actors will be required not only to have a great talent for acting but also a strong determination to succeed in the theater and motion pictures. They must be able to memorize hundreds of lines and should have a good speaking voice. The ability to sing and dance is important for increasing the opportunities for the young actor. Almost all actors are required to audition for a part before they receive the role. In film and television actors will generally complete screen tests to see how they appear on film. In all fields of acting, a love of performing is a must. It might take many years for an actor to achieve any success, if they achieve it at all.

Performers on the Broadway stage must be members of the Actors' Equity Association before being cast. While union membership may not always be required, many actors find it advantageous to belong to a union that covers their particular field of performing arts. These organizations include the Actors' Equity Association (stage), Screen Actors Guild or Screen Extras Guild (motion pictures and television films), or American Federation of Television and Radio Artists (TV, recording, and radio). In addition, some actors may benefit from membership in the American Guild of Variety Artists (nightclubs and so on), American Guild of Musical Artists (opera and ballet), or organizations such as the Hebrew Actors Union or Italian Actors Union for productions in those languages.

EXPLORING

The best way to explore this career is to participate in school or local theater productions. Even working on the props or lighting crew will provide insight into the field.

Also, attend as many dramatic productions as possible and try to talk with people who either are currently in the theater or have been at one time. They can offer advice to individuals interested in a career in the theater.

There are many books about acting that concern not only how to perform, but also the nature of the work, its offerings, advantages, and disadvantages.

EMPLOYERS

Motion pictures, television, and the stage are the largest fields of employment for actors, with television commercials representing as much as 60 percent of all acting jobs. Most of the opportunities for employment in these fields are either in Los Angeles or in New York. On the stage, even road shows often have their beginning in New York, with the selection of actors conducted there along with rehearsals. However, nearly every city and most communities present local and regional theater productions.

As cable-television networks continue to produce more and more of their own programs and films, they will become major providers of employment for actors. Home video will also continue to create new acting jobs, as will the music video business.

The lowest numbers of actors are employed by stage productions. In addition to Broadway shows and regional theater, there are employment opportunities for stage actors in summer stock, at resorts, and on cruise ships.

STARTING OUT

Probably the best way to enter acting is to start with high school, local, or college productions and to gain as much experience as possible on that level. Very rarely is an inexperienced actor given an opportunity to perform on stage or in a film in New York or Hollywood. The field is extremely difficult to enter; the more experience and ability beginners have, however, the greater the possibilities for entrance.

Those venturing to New York or Hollywood are encouraged first to have enough money to support themselves during the long waiting and searching period normally required before a job is found. Most will list themselves with a casting agency that will help them find a part as an extra or a bit player, either in theater or film. These agencies keep names on file along with photographs and a description of the individual's features and experience, and if a part comes along that may be suitable, they contact that person. Very often, however, names are added to their lists only when the number of people in a particular physical category is low. For instance, the agency may not have enough athletic young women on its roster, and if the applicant happens to fit this description, her name is added.

ADVANCEMENT

New actors will normally start with bit parts and will have only a few lines to speak, if any. The normal progression would then be landing larger supporting roles and then, in the case of theater, possibly a role as an understudy for one of the main actors. The understudy usually has an opportunity to fill in should the main actor be unable to give a performance. Many film and television actors get their start in commercials or by appearing in government and commercially sponsored public-service announcements, films, and programs. Other actors join the afternoon soap operas and continue on to evening programs. Many actors also have started in on-camera roles such as presenting the weather segment of a local news program. Once an actor has gained experience, he or she may go on to play stronger supporting roles or even leading roles in stage, television, or film productions. From there, an actor may go on to stardom. Only a very small number of actors ever reach that pinnacle, however.

Some actors eventually go into related occupations and become drama coaches, drama teachers, producers, stage directors, motion-picture directors, television directors, radio directors, stage managers, casting directors, or artist and repertoire managers. Others may combine one or more of these functions while continuing their careers.

EARNINGS

The wage scale for actors is largely controlled through bargaining agreements reached by various unions in negotiations with producers. These agreements normally control the minimum salaries, hours of work permitted per week, and other conditions of employment. In addition, each artist enters into a separate contract that may provide for higher salaries.

In 2003 the minimum daily salary of any member of the Screen Actors Guild (SAG) in a speaking role was $678, or $2,352 for a five-day workweek. Motion-picture actors may also receive additional payments known as residuals as part of their guaranteed salary. Many motion-picture actors receive residuals whenever films, TV shows, and

TV commercials in which they appear are rerun, sold for TV exhibition, or put on DVD. Residuals often exceed the actor's original salary and account for about one-third of all actors' income.

According to the Actors' Equity Association, the minimum weekly salary for actors in a Broadway production was $1,354 in 2003. Actors performing in off-Broadway performance had weekly salaries that ranged from $479 to $557 in 2003. Regional theaters that operate under Equity pay actors $531–$800 a week; those that tour with a show are given an extra $111 per week for living expenses.

According to the U.S. Department of Labor, the median yearly earning of all actors was $23,470 in 2002. The department also reported the lowest paid 10 percent earned less than $13,330 annually, while the highest paid 10 percent made more than $106,360.

The annual earnings of persons in television and movies are affected by frequent periods of unemployment. According to SAG, most of its members earn less than $5,000 a year from acting jobs. Unions offer health, welfare, and pension funds for members working more than a set number of weeks a year. Some actors are eligible for paid vacation and sick time, depending on the work contract.

In all fields, well-known actors have salary rates above the minimums, and the salaries of the few top stars are many times higher. Actors in television series may earn tens of thousands of dollars per week, while a few may earn as much as $1 million or more per week. Salaries for these actors vary considerably and are negotiated individually. In film, top stars may earn as much as $20 million per film, and, after receiving a percentage of the gross earned by the film, these stars can earn far, far more.

Until recent years, female film stars tended to earn lower salaries than their male counterparts; stars such as Julia Roberts, Jodie Foster, Halle Berry, and others have started to reverse that trend. The average annual earnings for all motion-picture actors, however, are usually low for all but the best-known performers because of the periods of unemployment.

WORK ENVIRONMENT

Actors work under varying conditions. Those employed in motion pictures may work in air-conditioned studios one week and be on location in a hot desert the next.

Those in stage productions perform under all types of conditions. The number of hours employed per day or week varies, as does the number of weeks employed per year. Stage actors normally perform eight shows per week with any additional performances paid for as overtime. The basic workweek after the show opens is about 36 hours unless major changes in the play are needed. The number of hours worked per week is considerably more before the opening because of rehearsals. Evening work is a natural part of a stage actor's life. Rehearsals often are held at night and over holidays and weekends. If the play goes on the road, much traveling will be involved.

A number of actors cannot receive unemployment compensation when they are waiting for their next part, primarily because they have not worked enough to meet the minimum eligibility requirements for compensation. Sick leaves and paid vacations are not usually available to the actor. However, union actors who earn the minimum qualifications now receive full medical and health insurance under all the actors' unions. Those who earn health-plan benefits for 10 years become eligible for a pension upon retirement. The acting field is very uncertain. Aspirants never know whether they will be able to get into the profession, and, once in, there are uncertainties as to whether the show will be well received and, if not, whether the actor's reputation can survive a badly received show.

OUTLOOK

Employment in acting is expected to grow at an average rate through 2012, according to the U.S. Department of Labor. Although people will always be attracted to this profession, and although there will always be positions available, many will pursue other career paths because of the fierce competition and relatively low pay. However, the growth of satellite and cable television in the past decade has created a demand for more actors, especially as the cable networks produce more and more of their own programs and films. The rise of home video and DVD has also created new acting jobs, as more and more films are made strictly for the home-video market. Many resorts built in the 1980s and 1990s present their own theatrical productions, providing more job opportunities for actors. Jobs in theater, however, face pressure as the cost of mounting a production increases and many nonprofit and smaller theaters lose their funding.

Despite the growth in opportunities, there are many more actors than there are roles, and this is likely to remain true for years to come. This is true in all areas of the arts, including radio, television, motion pictures, and theater, and even those who are employed are typically employed during only a small portion of the year. Many actors must supplement their income by working at other jobs, as secretaries, waiters, or taxi drivers, for example. Almost all performers are members of more than one union in order to take advantage of various opportunities as they become available.

It should be recognized that of the 105,000 or so actors in the United States today, a much smaller number are employed at any one time. Of these, few are able to support themselves on their earnings from acting, and fewer still will ever achieve stardom. Most actors work for many years before becoming known, and most of these do not rise above supporting roles. The vast majority of actors, meanwhile, are still looking for their big break. There are many more applicants in all areas than there are positions. As with most careers in the arts, people enter this one out of a genuine love for the field.

TO LEARN MORE ABOUT ACTORS

BOOKS

Bruder, Melissa. *A Practical Handbook for the Actor.* New York: Vintage, 1986.

Lee, Robert L. *Everything about Theater!: The Guidebook of Theater Fundamentals.* Colorado Springs, Colo.: Meriwether, 1996.

Quinlan, Kathryn A. *Actor.* Mankato, Minn.: Capstone Press, 1998.

Stevens, Chambers. *Magnificent Monologues for Kids.* South Pasadena, Calif.: Sandcastle, 1999.

WEBSITES AND ORGANIZATIONS

The Actors' Equity Association is a professional union for actors in theater and "live" industrial productions, stage managers, some directors, and choreographers.

Actors' Equity Association
165 West 46th Street
New York, NY 10036
Tel: 212-869-8530
E-mail: info@actorsequity.org
http://www.actorsequity.org

This union represents television and radio performers, including actors, announcers, dancers, disc jockeys, newspersons, singers, specialty acts, sportscasters, and stuntpersons.

American Federation of Television and
Radio Artists
260 Madison Avenue
New York, NY 10016
Tel: 212-532-0800
E-mail: aftra@aftra.com
http://www.aftra.com

A directory of theatrical programs may be purchased from National Association of Schools of Theater (NAST). For answers to a number of frequently asked questions concerning education, visit the NAST website.

National Association of Schools of Theater (NAST)

11250 Roger Bacon Drive, Suite 21

Reston, VA 20190

Tel: 703-437-0700

E-mail: info@arts-accredit.org

http://www.arts-accredit.org/nast

The Screen Actors Guild (SAG) provides general information on actors, directors, and producers. Visit the SAG website for more information.

Screen Actors Guild (SAG)

5757 Wilshire Boulevard

Los Angeles, CA 90036

Tel: 323-954-1600

http://www.sag.com

For information about opportunities in not-for-profit theaters, contact the Theatre Communications Group.

Theatre Communications Group

355 Lexington Avenue

New York, NY 10017

Tel: 212-697-5230

E-mail: tcg@tcg.org

http://www.tcg.org

This site has information for beginners on acting and the acting business.

Acting Workshop On-Line

http://www.redbirdstudio.com/AWOL/acting2.html

HOW TO BECOME A PRODUCER

THE JOB

The primary role of a producer is to organize and secure the financial backing necessary to undertake a motion picture project. The director, by contrast, creates the film from the screenplay. Despite this general distinction, the producer often takes part in creative decisions, and occasionally one person is both the producer and director. On some small projects, such as a nature or historical documentary for a public-television broadcast, the producer might also be the writer and cameraman.

The job of a producer generally begins in the preproduction stage of filmmaking with the selection of a movie idea from a script or other material. Some films are made from original screenplays, while others are adapted from books. If a book is selected, the producer must first purchase the rights from the author or his or her publishing company, and a writer must be hired to adapt the book into a screenplay format. Producers are usually inundated with scripts from writers and others who have ideas for a movie. Producers may have their own ideas for a motion picture and will hire a writer to write the screenplay. Occasionally a studio will approach a producer, typically a producer who has had many commercially or artistically successful films in the past, with a project.

After selecting a project, the producer will find a director, the technical staff, and the leading actor or actors to participate in the film. Along with the script and screenwriter, these essential people are referred to as the *package*. Packaging is sometimes arranged with the help of talent agencies. It is the package that the producer tries to sell to an investor to obtain the necessary funds to finance the salaries and cost of the film.

There are three common sources for financing a film: major studios, production companies, and individual investors. A small number of producers have enough money to pay for their own projects. Major studios are the largest source of money, and they finance most of the big-budget films. Although some studios have full-time producers on staff, they hire self-employed, or independent producers, for many projects. Large production companies often have the capital resources to fund projects that they feel will be commercially successful. On the smaller end of the scale, producers of documentary films commonly approach individual donors; foundations; art agencies of federal, state, and local governments; and even family members and churches. The National Endowment for the Humanities and the National Endowment for the Arts are major federal benefactors of cinema.

Raising money from individual investors can occupy much of the producer's time. Fund-raising may be done on the telephone, as well as in conferences, business lunches, and even at parties. The producer may also look for a distributor for the film even before the production begins.

Obtaining the necessary financing does not guarantee a film will be made. After raising the money, the producer takes the basic plan of the package and tries to work it into a developed project. The script may be rewritten several times, the full cast of actors is hired, salaries are negotiated, and logistical problems, such as the location of the filming, are worked out. On some projects it might be the director who handles these tasks, or the director may work with the producer. Most major film projects do not get beyond this complicated stage of development.

During the production phase, the producer tries to keep the project on schedule and the spending within the established budget. Other production tasks include the review of dailies, which are the prints of the day's filming. As the head of the project, the producer is ultimately responsible for resolving all problems, including conflicts such as those between the director and an actor, and the director and the studio. If the film is successfully completed, the producer monitors its distribution and may participate in the publicity and advertising of the film.

To accomplish the many and varied tasks the position requires, producers hire a number of subordinates, such as associate producers, sometimes called coproducers, line producers, and production assistants. Job titles, however, vary from project to project. In general, associate producers work directly under the producer and oversee the major areas of the project, such as the budget. Line producers handle the day-to-day operations of the project. Production assistants may perform substantive tasks, such as reviewing scripts, but others are hired to run errands. Another title, executive producer, often refers to the person who puts up the money, such as a studio executive, but it is sometimes an honorary title with no functional relevance to the project.

REQUIREMENTS

There is no minimum educational requirement for becoming a producer. Many producers, however, are college graduates, and many also have a business degree or other previous business experience. They must not only be talented salespeople and administrators but also have a thorough understanding of film and motion-picture technology. Such understanding, of course, only comes from experience.

High School

High school courses that will be of assistance to you in your work as a producer include speech, mathematics, business, psychology, and English.

Postsecondary Training

Formal study of film, television, communications, theater, writing, English literature, or art is helpful, as the producer must have the background to know whether an idea or script is worth pursuing. Many entry-level positions in the film industry are given to people who have studied liberal arts, cinema, or both.

In the United States there are more than 1,000 colleges, universities, and trade schools that offer classes in film or television studies; more than 120 of these offer undergraduate programs, and more than 50 grant master's degrees. A small number of Ph.D. programs also exist.

Graduation from a film or television course of study does not guarantee employment in the industry. Some programs are quite expensive, costing more than $50,000 in tuition alone for three years of study. Others do not have the resources to allow all students to make their own films.

Programs in Los Angeles and New York, the major centers of the entertainment industry, may provide the best opportunities for making contacts that can be of benefit when seeking employment.

Other Requirements

Producers come from a wide variety of backgrounds. Some start out as magazine editors, business-school graduates, actors, or secretaries, messengers, and production assistants for a film studio. Many have never formally studied film.

Most producers, however, get their position through several years of experience in the industry, perseverance, and a keen sense for what projects will be artistically and commercially successful.

EXPLORING

There are many ways to gain experience in filmmaking. Some high schools have film and video clubs, for example, or courses on the use of motion-picture equipment. Experience in high school or college theater can also be useful. One of the best ways to gain experience is to volunteer for a student or low-budget film project; positions on such projects are often advertised in local trade publications. Community cable stations also hire volunteers and may even offer internships.

EMPLOYERS

Many producers in the field are self-employed. Others are salaried employees of film companies, television networks, and television stations. The greatest concentration of motion picture producers is in Hollywood and New York. Hollywood alone has more than 2,000 producers.

STARTING OUT

Becoming a producer is similar to becoming president of a company. Unless a person is independently wealthy and can finance whichever projects he or she chooses, prior experience in the field is necessary. Because there are so few positions, even with experience it is extremely difficult to become a successful producer.

Most motion-picture producers have attained their position only after years of moving up the industry ladder. Thus, it is important to concentrate on immediate goals, such as getting an entry-level position in a film company. Some enter the field by getting a job as a production assistant. An entry-level production assistant may photocopy the scripts for actors to use, assist in setting up equipment, or perform other menial tasks, often for very little or even no pay. While a production assistant's work is often tedious and of seemingly little reward, it nevertheless does expose one to the intricacies of filmmaking and, more important, creates an opportunity to make contacts with others in the industry.

Those interested in the field should approach film companies, television stations, or the television networks about employment opportunities as a production assistant. Small television stations often provide the best opportunity for those who are interested in television production. Positions may also be listed in trade publications.

ADVANCEMENT

There is little room for advancement because producers are at the top of their profession. Advancement for producers is generally measured by the types of projects they do, increased earnings, and respect in the field. At television stations, a producer can advance to program director. Some producers become directors or make enough money to finance their own projects.

EARNINGS

Producers are generally paid a percentage of the project's profits or a fee negotiated between the producer and a studio. The U.S. Department of Labor reports that producers and directors earned average salaries of $46,240 in 2002. Salaries ranged from less than $23,300 to more than $119,760. Producers of highly successful films can earn $200,000 or more, while those who make low-budget or documentary films might earn considerably less than the average. In general, producers in the film industry earn more than television producers. The U.S. Department of Labor reports that producers employed in the motion-picture industry had average earnings of $56,090 in 2002, while those employed in television broadcasting averaged $38,480.

WORK ENVIRONMENT

Producers have greater control over their working conditions than most other people working in the motion-picture industry do. They may have the autonomy of choosing their own projects, setting their own hours, and delegating duties to others as necessary. The work often brings considerable personal satisfaction. But it is not without constraints. Producers must work within a stressful schedule complicated by competing work pressures and often-daily crises. Each project brings a significant financial and professional risk. Long hours and weekend work are common. Most producers must provide for their own health insurance and other benefits.

OUTLOOK

Employment for producers is expected to grow about as fast as the average through 2012, according to the U.S. Department of Labor. Though opportunities may increase with the expansion of cable and satellite television, news programs, DVD rentals, and an increased overseas demand for American-made films, competition for jobs will be high. Live theater and entertainment will also provide job openings. Some positions will be available as current producers leave the workforce.

TO LEARN MORE ABOUT PRODUCERS

BOOKS

Erickson, Gunnar, Mark Halloran, and Harris Tulchin. *The Independent Film Producer's Survival Guide: A Business and Legal Sourcebook.* New York: Omnibus Press, 2002.

Harmon, Renee. *The Beginning Filmmaker's Business Guide: Financial, Legal, Marketing, and Distribution Basics of Making Movies.* New York: Walker & Company, 1993.

Houghton, Buck. *What a Producer Does: The Art of Moviemaking (Not the Business).* Los Angeles: Silman-James Press, 1991.

Levy, Frederick. *Hollywood 101: The Film Industry.* Renaissance Books, 2000.

Rensin, David. *The Mailroom: Hollywood History from the Bottom Up.* New York: Random House, 2003.

WEBSITES AND ORGANIZATIONS

Visit the Producers Guild of America (PGA) website to read an online version of *Point of View* magazine, which focuses on the role of producers in the motion picture and television industries.

Producers Guild of America (PGA)

8530 Wilshire Boulevard, Suite 450

Beverly Hills, CA 90211

http://www.producersguild.org

The Broadcast Education Association is a good source of information on scholarships and grants, interest divisions, and filmmaking publications.

Broadcast Education Association

1771 N Street, NW

Washington, DC 20036

http://www.beaweb.org

TO LEARN MORE ABOUT DENZEL WASHINGTON

BOOKS

Brode, Douglas. *Denzel Washington: His Films and Career.* New York: Kensington, 1996.

Graham, Judith, Hilary D. Claggett, Elizabeth A. Schick, Miriam Helbok, eds. *Current Biography Yearbook 1992.* Bronx, N.Y.: H. W. Wilson, 1992.

Hill, Anne E. *Denzel Washington.* Philadelphia: Chelsea House, 1999.*

Jenkins, Barbara Williams, and Jessie Carney Smith. "Denzel Washington," in *Notable Black American Men.* Detroit: Gale Group, 1999.

Kram, Mark. "Denzel Washington," in *Contemporary Black Biography, Vol. 16*. Detroit: Gale Group, 1998.

Nickson, Chris. *Denzel Washington*. New York: St. Martin's, 1996.

Parish, James Robert. *Today's Black Hollywood*. New York: Kensington, 1995.

Parish, James Robert, and Allan Taylor, eds. *The Encyclopedia of Ethnic Groups in Hollywood*. New York: Facts On File, 2002.

Simmons, Alex. *Denzel Washington*. Austin, Tex.: Steck-Vaughn, 1998.*

Wheeler, Jill C. *Denzel Washington.* Minneapolis: Abdo, 2002.*

Wooten, Sara McIntosh. *Denzel Washington: Academy Award–Winning Actor*. Berkeley Heights, N.J: Enslow, 2003.*

* Young adult book

MAGAZINES

Cawley, Janet. "Denzel Washington: Destined for Greatness." *Biography*, March 2002.

Fleming, Michael, "Denzel Washington." *Playboy*, December 2002.

Greenfield, Jeff. "In His Stars." *Reader's Digest*, December 2002.

Smith, Sean M. "Denzel Washington." *Premiere*, October 2002.

WEBSITES

E! online

http://www.eonline.com

Internet Movie Database

http://www.imdb.com

Boys and Girls Clubs of America

http://www.bgca.org/

INDEX

Page numbers in *italics* indicate illustrations.

ABOUT THE AUTHOR

James Robert Parish, a former entertainment reporter, publicist, and book-series editor, is the author of numerous biographies and reference books of the entertainment industry including *Halle Berry: Actor, Stephen King: Writer, Tom Hanks: Actor, Steven Spielberg: Filmmaker, Whitney Houston, The Hollywood Book of Love, Hollywood Divas, Hollywood Bad Boys, The Encyclopedia of Ethnic Groups in Hollywood, Jet Li, Jason Biggs, Gus Van Sant, The Hollywood Book of Death, Whoopi Goldberg, Rosie O'Donnell's Story, The Unofficial "Murder, She Wrote" Casebook, Today's Black Hollywood, Let's Talk! America's Favorite TV Talk Show Hosts, Black Action Pictures, Liza Minnelli, The Elvis Presley Scrapbook,* and *Hollywood's Great Love Teams.*

Mr. Parish is a frequent on-camera interviewee on cable and network TV for documentaries on the performing arts both in the United States and in the United Kingdom. He resides in Studio City, California.